THE PURPOSE OF LIFE

An Eastern Philosophical Vision

Carlo Filice

D1431785

45.46

University Press of America,® Inc.
Lanham · Boulder · New York · Toronto · Plymouth, UK

Library of Congress Control Number: 2011929057
ISBN: 978-0-7618-5582-8 (paperback : alk. paper)
eISBN: 978-0-7618-5583-5

To my wife, Karen

CONTENTS

CONTENTS (Cont)

CONTENTS (Cont)

PREFACE

We humans believe in and do crazy things. But we are not dummies. We often display common sense, and wondrous intelligence.

At our best, our imagination can soar.

At our best, we know what really matters.

Our knowledge of what matters combined with our imagination will guide the following fable. This fable is an attempt to shed light on the disputed realm of ultimate meaning.

Our goal is nothing short of grasping the purpose of it all!

At the center of the fable is the philosophical game of imagining being a god.

Can we fruitfully play at being a god? We will have to see.

Playing at being a god is a serious game, but it is only a game. If we lose, we can always fall back on traditional answers, or non-answers, regarding the purpose of it all.

However, we should not sell ourselves short. We can do more than we generally think!

1
Why?

My mom just died. Rheumatoid arthritis and strokes whittled her down. Her life has been difficult and unfulfilled. My wife lost her parents when they were in their fifties. Cancer. One of my friends, Tom Lapic, died in his forties in a plane crash. He died at the moment when his life had finally turned favorably.

Virtually everyone who lives a long time loses loved ones. Some of our loved ones die very prematurely. Outside of our personal sphere, which can occasionally be very fortunate, millions of children continue to be born in misery and disease on our planet. Many of them never get a real shot at life.

Most unsettling of all, of course, is the fact that our own current lives will come to an end—mine as well as yours. Even happy people will die at some point, even if not prematurely.

Death is natural. Yet, it is puzzling and sad. Most of us wish to continue our conscious existence.

Yes, severe infirmities and chronic suffering can outweigh this wish. But infirmities and suffering do not render neutral the value of continued awareness, feeling, and doing.

When deaths are premature and miseries undeserved things get even more disturbing.

The sadness and perplexity we feel in the face of these disturbing facts derive from two things: the undeniable value of our existence, and the expectation that existence be morally fair.

It is because we humans, as well as many non-humans, matter that the brute facts of mortality, fragility, accidents, disease, cruelties, earthquakes, unfair beginnings, abrupt endings… give us pause. It is because of these brute and disturbing facts that we seek a big purpose that would make sense of them.

Are lives here for a purpose? Why is the world set up as it is, and not differently?

The answers will have to deal with values and reasons. Such answers will also depend on how we deal with the most basic and puzzling of all questions: why is there a world at all instead of nothing?

We are startled at the thought, when it periodically hits us, that we and the world exist at all. Philosophers like Wittgenstein have termed the sheer fact of existence the most mystical of all facts.

Perhaps if we can shed light on this most mystical of all facts, we might also shed light on the morally puzzling features of our world. Knowing why the world is here could help us to know why it's set up as it is. This in turn should help us explain death, senseless deaths, and inauspicious births.

We will suggest that questions regarding the very existence of our world, on the one hand, and questions regarding value and fairness, on the other, are related.

Perhaps there is something, as opposed to nothing, because ultimately some things matter. Perhaps ultimate value explains our existence.

This friendly, but not modest, suggestion will be the basis for our fable.

2
Basic questions and basic answers

We cannot avoid basic questions regarding overall life purposes.

The lives of thoughtful people swing from nearly complete immersion in tasks at hand, to puzzled wonderment at being consciously alive and at the fact that that we won't always be. At one moment all that counts is finishing the current work project, steering our car through heavy traffic, winning this tennis point, lending a hand to our neighbor. Then at a later moment we stand bemused at the seriousness with which we take the small things of everyday life.

There is no doubt that we derive satisfaction and meaning from many activities in which we are immersed. Teaching young people and listening to music are examples. We can easily imagine living an overall meaningful, satisfying, and happy life. Countless people, from Aristotle to Lao Tze, have written on how to do this. Current research on the psychology of happiness has much to impart on living well. Flow activities and acts of kindness, for instance, make our lives happier.

However, the satisfaction of living well is not enough. Life remains generally precarious. Even if we are among the lucky ones to lead fulfilling lives, what about the Tom Lapics who did just about everything right and yet are cut down prematurely? What about the mothers and children who did not get a fair shake in life? What about mortality itself?

We simply need a big purpose, one tied to some big picture, to make sense of these things.

Why have lives at all, particularly ones like ours with acute inner consciousnesses, if they are so finite and so seemingly chancy and unfair? Why do lives, human and non-human, begin in conditions of drastically unequal opportunities? Why is there so much seemingly undeserved suffering in this world? There are, of course, two broad answers to these types of questions:

Answer 1: Nobody promised us a rose garden or a fair existence or an infinite one! Lives are the result of blind natural processes, with no ultimate purposes. The obstinate tendencies of individuals, species, or genes, to survive and reproduce—as well as to die—do not serve some other goal. The survival tendencies are simply there. These tendencies are there by accident, and are of neutral value.

Much of modern science suggests this type of answer.

We will say only a little here about this general view. It might be true. Yet, our inner being revolts against this view. More importantly, there is no strong reason compelling us to accept this view.

Answer 2: Things did not just happen! Lives are the result of some intention that is in some sense prior to, and the source of, our universe. Life-forms are part of a wider reality, and of a bigger plan, and may not be so ultimately finite. Their existence was motivated, and has justification.

Most religious views suggest this second answer.

The goal in what follows is to bring out a sensible version of this second view. We will take advantage of a deep intuition behind religious impulses, namely, that things ultimately make sense. We will, however, steer away from the mumbo-jumbo that often accompanies those same religions. The ones we accidentally inherit, like my Catholicism, will receive no favoritism here.

Intelligence and a sense of fairness will be our guides.

Many theologians, philosophers, poets, and visionaries have provided the pieces of a sensible big picture. It is a matter of putting these pieces together in the right way, by highlighting many things we already know.

But we must look with care, and broadly.

3
The scientific no-purpose view

Much of our current thinking must meet with the approval of science. Scientists are the new theologians. They generally stress that reality as we now encounter it is the unintended product of physical processes. These processes may be lawful, regular, and understandable. But they are blind. Physical processes may or may not be in principle predictable. Either way, they have no overall meaning or goal.

Science understands best on physicalist models—that is, on models assuming that everything consists of material components, energy included. Even the sciences dealing without inner lives and our actions, such as psychology, would like to reduce our experiences to physical processes. Neuroscience is the hope here.

The attraction of science, as currently conceived, is based on its stunning technologies. These are, in turn, based on mathematically precise understanding of physical laws. Science yields technology that can make huge and heavy machines fly, and that can transmit pictures and sounds simultaneously across the planet.

Yet we must keep in mind that the view that "all is physical" is not itself a scientific view. It is a broader *philosophical* view, and one that is often simply presupposed in our scientific age.

In fact, we must admit that science cannot account for important factors in our common reality. Nothing spooky need be implied here. We are talking about the presence of our own consciousness, of meaning, of free will, of value, of beauty, of love bonds, of dreams. This list does not even include various intimations of uncanny things, such as signs of telepathic communications and of previous or of post-life existences.

Philosophers of late have been trying to give science-friendly accounts of the factors just listed: of consciousness, free will, dreams, beauty, etc. They have been trying to do so cleverly and with a touch of desperation. Many are lending a theoretical hand to viewing these phenomena as nothing more than fancy physical processes.

Some philosophers have even argued that consciousness itself is a kind of illusion. A similar fate has befallen free will: it is either treated as an illusion, or it is redefined to make it compatible with physicalist processes. Elsewhere, evolutionary psychologists have been trying to explain all human propensities, such as humor, music, philosophizing, beauty, by appealing to the survival-value of such activities.

Needless to say, these projects have left most people unconvinced. This is not for lack of effort and intellectual acumen. It is because they are lost causes!

Consciousness and beauty remain as real and as mysterious as ever. Free will and responsibility don't really fit in our scientific picture of the universe, yet we cannot wish them away. Dreams remain just plain weird—and no explanation has even come close to making sense of their presence and nature.

There is more. We have cathedrals, innate musical geniuses, the depths of love, the joy of playing sports, humor. These and other commonplace phenomena simply escape the narrow boundaries of material explanations. The survival-based explanations of behavioral scientists may even have things backwards.

Perhaps we don't enjoy play and great music because these indirectly help us to survive. Perhaps we seek to survive so as to play and to enjoy great music! Do birds play to better survive? Or do they seek to survive so as to play? .

Physicalist science is great at what it does. But there are things that it cannot be asked to do. It can enable music to be heard great distances from where it occurs. It can understand wave properties of sound. It cannot, however, understand the quality of great music by analyzing its physical sound-components. It cannot understand the smell and visual beauty of roses by examining the chemistry of the petals.

We would be wise not to trust physicalist science alone to give us a complete picture of reality. It does provide tools for a better life. It understands the principles that make these tools work. It does not, however, have tools for explaining the better, the worse, and the meaningful. When it judges that reality is ultimately pointless, we need not jump to attention.

4
The possible meaning of it all

We are going to put physicalism and purposelessness aside.

A complete view of the universe will include scientific accounts of physical dimensions of reality. But a correct view must also account for other dimensions of reality dealing with inner lives and value phenomena.

Many learned colleagues will disagree here. It is difficult to blame them, given centuries of advances of science in countless areas. We will invite them to treat what follows as a fable, or as hypothetical account. This is how the world would have to be if it were to make ultimate sense.

So, we begin by noting the presence of mysterious and value-carrying dimensions, like consciousness and natural beauty. We suggest that these point at a purpose behind the presence of everything.

Without an overall purpose, our consciousnesses and our civilizations would be beautiful but ephemeral flames that last an instant only to fall back into cosmic darkness. There must be more to the universe, reality, our earthly lives, my mom's and your mom's lives, Tom Lapic's life.

For reality and our lives to have a big purpose, it must have been planned or intended. This intention, if we could know it, should shed light on why we are here and on what we as humans should be doing.

An intention behind the cosmos in turn implies a consciousness or a powerful mind. Such a mind must be a kind of super-consciousness, or super-gestalt-of-consciousnesses, or even many of these, to intend it. We can call such a super-consciousness a god. We don't have to build much into this term yet. There might also be many such gods.

Gods that intend this world must have wanted to achieve some end.

A divine intention need not be as simple as our intentions. It would be surprising if it were. Nonetheless it must be relatable to ours, or else it would not be an intention at all. In particular, an intention must come from some inner consciousness, and must aim at some outcome.

Purposes and intentions need a consciousness because only consciousnesses can point directly at what is outside themselves. Signs and words and even events can point at things outside themselves, but only indirectly. They need to be interpreted by consciousnesses. An arrow-sign is merely a mark on some surface if no mind is there to read it as a signal with meaning that points at something else.

If an inner consciousness, an inner god, is the source of the cosmic intention behind the universe, then something in this source must have yearned for an externalized universe, or for many universes. There must have been a *motive*.

Our reality could not have been an after-thought, an uncontrolled movement, a random divine sneezing. There is too much order, lawfulness, complexity, beauty, size, diversification, for our world to have been an accident.

Above all, there is the mystery and wonder of our own inner lives. There isn't just an orderly world, but one with weird and precious consciousnesses in it. It could have been a zombie world, but it is not.

⌈No random divine sneezing could produce this special world!⌋

How do you know? (handwritten margin note)

Yes, there is also a tendency in this world toward inertia, dissolution, destruction. These are indeed challenges for overall purposiveness. We will have to address them.

For now, we will start with one idea: if there had to be a divine motive for our world, such a motive would be the clue to the meaning of it all.

5
Divine motives

We note, then, that an overall purpose for the universe rests on some motive of some divine super-mind.

Our own Abrahamic religions, Christianity included, have not been very helpful as to motive. At times they have professed our incapacity in the face of these big questions, because the divine transcends our intellectual powers. At times Abrahamic traditions ask us simply to trust that their god has good reasons for the universe and our role in it. At other times they have attributed "creation" to an overflow of divine goodness.

We are going to stubbornly insist that our imaginative and intellectual powers can grasp ultimate ends, or at least some of them. We insist on this because we possess a good idea of *intrinsic* values, as we will see, and these values are ultimate ends. Intrinsic values are values that cannot be reduced to more basic values or to non-values. They are not local prejudices.

If some values are really intrinsic and ultimate, then even the gods would have to respond to them.

We are also going to take the view that the goodness-overflow theory is at best incomplete. It is simplistic, and a touch moralistic. It tends to focus on benevolence and on love connections. These are important, but narrow. If goodness is, however, interpreted broadly to mean value generally, then we'll agree with it.

Benevolence and love connections, as treated in Abrahamic traditions, are connections involving mainly humans and gods (or one god). Love bonds involving non-human animals are left out.

The focus of creation is the moral testing of humans, in these traditions. This narrow circle of moral concern, in Abrahamic traditions, leaves out the entire world of animal suffering. Lambs and rams have been seen as sacrificial tools to appease and thank the gods. These animals, and similar others, are still treated merely as human food in predominantly Abrahamic countries.

Moreover, the vastness of the universe is treated as mere background for such human tests. Even if a more inclusive version of love and beneficence were adopted, it would ignore other worthy aspects of our universe. Why have billions of immense galaxies, and billions of earth years, if all that was needed is a local tiny environment for the moral testing of one species?

Besides, our little earth alone has too much of value that cannot be captured by the moral sphere. There is the joy of kids playing soccer. There is the rambunctiousness of birds chasing each other. There is the creation of great poems and of melancholy music. There is the blossoming of flowers.

Buddhist traditions do have a more inclusive moral focus, making all suffering a matter of concern irrespective of species. However, these traditions also are of no help with cosmic motives. Why are we, and all sentient beings, caught in the presumed wheel of suffering and "samsara" in the first place? No answer seems available here.

Hindu mystics may have come closest to an answer, by alluding to a primordial being (Brahman) multiplying itself into the many-ness of the world.

But why did such a Hindu super-deity do so? Partly out of play, according to influential Hindu theologians like Shankara. This is not as foolish as it sounds, since the playful can include the tragic and the non-human.

Still, this motive remains a little too whimsical. For one thing, not all play is fair play.

What if we combined this Hindu tale of a playful god who takes the form of the universe, with the Abrahamic idea of divine goodness, and with an expanded conception of value?

What follows is a fable inspired by this kind of composite view.

6
Value as the key to it all

In looking for divine reasons and purposes, we should start from the most evident observations. All the beings we know act in pursuit of things they value. Bees pursue flowers. Children pursue play. Adults pursue love and wealth. All pursue the company of others.

We could say, instead, that all beings pursue things they merely want—and that what they want is arbitrary or of neutral value. They want what they want just because they do.

But conscious beings don't just want things arbitrarily. They want things and states of being that matter to them. They want these things or states because they perceive them as having value. Freedom, as an example, is not great because we want it. We want it because we simply find it to be great. We might even die for it.

Do we want things like freedom because it has proven of survival value? No doubt that this is partly so, but why do we seek to survive? Our experience shows that we seek to survive because things like freedom, fun, and friends have value. When these things can no longer be appreciated the urge to survive also vanishes.

Could value be the driving factor behind divine motivation? Might there be value-things that even a super-god must honor? Perhaps some things must be valued by anyone who is capable of valuing them.

If some things must be so valued, surely gods would value them, since gods must have the capacities for valuing them.

We must be careful to avoid mere wishful thinking here. Yet, we must also notice that we ourselves have little choice in basic value matters. We cannot help but value movement, roses, music, and adventure. The gods might also be subject to the pull of value, though no doubt value covering a much wider spectrum.

It turns out, as we will see, that this is likely the case. Certain kinds of value simply demand recognition. Once we see this, we will see that an "original" divine purpose has to be linked with producing, fulfilling, and enhancing these kinds of value.

What kinds of value demand recognition?

Let's begin by looking at our ordinary values. What do we seek? We strive, we study, we work… to get things like money. We do so to stay alive, yes, but also to have more options, and to grow flowers or play tennis. We seek to help others so that they too can grow flowers or play tennis. We seek vacations for the sake of new sights, or new adventures, or more sunshine. We seek companionship and love. Some of us even study or work simply for the love of knowledge, of building, of healing, or of teaching.

Let's focus on some of the simpler payoffs, like basking in the sun or playing tennis or traveling or growing flowers. They are payoffs partly because they are satisfying, fulfilling, fun. The fun of playing tennis is tied to, or consists of, having experiences that matter for their own sake. Hitting a solid tennis shot is fun. Overcoming resistance is fun. The sensation of being bathed by sunshine simply feels good.

Feeling good and having fun matter in themselves. These experiences are of intrinsic value.

Similar things can be said for our encounters with roses, music, cats, and other people; or of our acts of playing, building, and reading. Feeling good, fun, warmth, satisfaction, are involved somewhere in these pursuits.

The key point is that basic things like fun and feeling good must be recognized as values. They have a sort of *self-mattering* quality. We pursue what is fun for its own sake, or simply because it is fun.

Fun and feeling good are not all that self-matters. Other basic states, like remaining consciously alive and remaining free, also have this self-mattering quality. We want these states for their own sake.

If nothing mattered (to us or anyone) in this way and for its own sake, irreducibly, nothing would matter indirectly to anyone either. We would have no reason to move, to act, or to do dull tasks. We seek survival because some things matter for their own sake, intrinsically.

We do what we do because either the doing itself, or the result, in some way satisfies us directly. Value-things, value-states, things that self-matter—these make up the engine and fuel of our being!

7

The gods must recognize value

We have tentatively seen that in our case intrinsic value fuels our motivational engine. Would value also fuel the motives of higher beings like gods? We must dare to say, Yes.

What else could prompt gods into action? Let's imagine the alternatives. Suppose divine activity is not prompted by value. What then? Either it is not prompted at all; or it is prompted by non-value, by what does not matter; or divine activity is accidental. Divine activity, then, would be either absent or arbitrary.

Since there is at least one universe to be accounted for, some divine activity has occurred or occurs. But why?

Did the gods act, but without any ultimate reason? Were they prompted to act by what does not matter?

If nothing self-matters, then any "initial" divine act would have been as worthy as any other, even from a divine point of view. Divine action itself would then be no more worthy than non-action. If nothing mattered for the gods in the first place, not even their own pleasure or bliss, then they would have no stimulus for doing anything.

They would not even have a stimulus for inventing values. Any intentional invention of value needs some pre-existing and beginningless values.

Might the value-invention have happened in a divine psyche by accident, with values arbitrarily chosen? Might this accident then have awakened the divine engine into action?

This possibility would make the "initial" active life of gods not only arbitrary but also curiously uncontrolled. Sure, we want some things, like love, to be uncontrolled in some ways. We want love to overtake us independently of our will. But love's object must not be completely random. A person who inexplicably comes to love only something trivial, like the ink of writing pens, and is indifferent to the suffering of others, is not a creature we would aspire to be.

If unworthy of us, we can safely infer that completely arbitrary and uncontrolled activity must be also unworthy of super beings like gods. Nor can the gods be "initially" moved by some internal value-neutral programming. Divine actions would then be caused, even compelled, but in a way that amounts to a blind spurring. It would be causation without justification.

Gods, more than us, must do what they do freely and for good reasons. Values provide the reasons.

Plato had arrived at the same conclusion long ago. Values must be ultimates. From the very "beginning" the gods must do what they do for good reasons. The goodness of these reasons must be independent of the gods themselves, and of their will.

Ok, we think that gods should be utterly unconstrained. If independent and intrinsic value drives their behavior, wouldn't gods be unduly constrained? Wouldn't intrinsic values interfere with divine freedom?

It is tempting to think so.

However, we have seen that a divine agent unbounded in its behavior by the good, by what counts, by value, either remains unmoved, or else moves for bad or arbitrary reasons. None of these options are worthy of a god.

We must insist that freedom does not mean arbitrariness.

We must insist that divine behavior is bounded by what a Platonist would call "the good."

8
Freedom is not arbitrariness

We have dared to claim that even a worthy god must move in accord with value. Value, in turn, must rest on a base of intrinsic values.

The worry remains that gods so construed would lack the complete freedom one expect of gods.

This worry, however, is based on a false notion of freedom as motivational arbitrariness.

We must see that value-boundaries are not constraints on an agent. Value-boundaries are the conditions for action in the first place. They are certainly the conditions for great actions.

Let's consider the example of musical value. Is the musician constrained by having to produce musical value, or good music? Would there even be musicians without such value? Does the need to produce good music limit or, instead, prompt music making?

Clearly, musical value is what prompts music-making in the first place.

Should we be concerned that the presence of intrinsic musical value will limit music possibilities? Have we mined and exhausted musical possibilities after creating millions of songs and symphonies and operas, and after doing so for centuries if not millennia?

History indicates otherwise. We keep creating new songs, new arrangements, new melodies, new genres of music, new musical instruments. The possibilities seem limitless.

Let's apply this point to the gods. Imagine that they face from the very "beginning" an array of platonic value-standards: from musical ones to moral ones to ones involved in visual beauty, to many other value standards we humans can hardly imagine. Some value standards may elude our grasp because they belong to worlds of non-space-time.

Let's also imagine that at the "beginning" such values standards exist at a general level, and are not actualized. They are waiting for appropriate worlds in which they will take concrete forms. Beauty might be an example of a generic value, which can only be expressed in forms that presuppose specific media. Visual beauty, for example, presupposes material forms. Caravaggio's and Picasso's paintings need a physical world. Similar things can be said for musical beauty. However, some beauty forms of expressions might require different worlds—ones beyond our current comprehension.

So, let's say that divine behavior is prompted and governed by a multitude of value standards, and by their need of specific forms of actualization in. If so, would divine behavior be unfree or confined?

If musical value alone does not confine, then how could a large spectrum of value-standards confine?

Standards would not confine at any level. Value-boundaries are no boundaries at all! They are only boundaries for meaningful and great action. Assembling a sequence of sounds only makes music if the sequence is guided by a sense of musical beauty.

Even for gods, then, value-standards would be an array of ultimate conditions for great and divine-worthy action.

No great action is possible without independent greatness standards.

Moreover, we have seen that value is necessary as motivation for divine action. What else could shake a god from a possible divine paralysis?

9

Worlds as entertainment value

We have seen that gods must be neither paralyzed nor arbitrary in their actions. Values provide the reasons for divine action. A divine consciousness would be moved by its natural recognition of value.

Which value would have to be so recognized?

Let us begin with the most basic ones.

We have already mentioned conscious existence and fun as self-mattering values.

The gods, let's presume, are in some sense immortals. As such, they would have their own conscious existence guaranteed. So, they would not have to seek it.

But conscious existence alone, mere empty consciousness, even if possible could not be fully satisfying. A god, let's presume again, has many super powers, including knowledge ones. Thus, a god would be aware of possibilities, including possibilities of an *enhanced existence*. An enhanced existence is a value-enriched one.

The gods would certainly be aware of values, or at least value-potentials, and of the possibilities of actualizing such values.

Even gods who "started out" as merely conscious would naturally seek their own value-enriched existence.

The pursuit of a value-enriched divine existence could then pave the way for the production of worlds.

How else to actualize values, if not through settings called worlds? How to achieve fun, beauty, and adventure, without some vehicle or setting in which to have fun or beauty or adventure?

Worlds, like ours, could then be vehicles for some forms of divine value-enhancement. The gods might, minimally, invent worlds simply for their own fun! We do something similar when we invent virtual or fictional worlds.

Fun does enrich one's existence.

Let's say, then, that the gods begin, fable-like, by seeking to enhance their "initial" empty conscious awareness. So they invent worlds for fun.

What kind of worlds would gods invent? What kind of worlds would generate a lot of fun, or even the most fun?

Here is a startling possibility.

Perhaps worlds that will yield the most fun and compelling enrichment for gods are worlds that necessarily acquire independent value. Then, once such invented worlds have independent value-status, even the gods would have to respect these worlds, and treat them accordingly! Perhaps the force of value will turn gods into moral agents.

We will see that this is in fact a very probable line of development.

The need to respect these worlds will, in turn, serve to endow the centers of value in these worlds—the conscious lives—with fairness and purpose.

Our own lives would be among the ones endowed with fairness and purpose.

This may look like a fairy tale. But as we develop it, we will see that it might be more than a fairy tale.

10
Entertainment value leads to other forms of value

So, then, we have imagined gods who "begin" as merely present. We then imagine them to follow their value-enrichment impulse, and thus to seek a minimal basic value: entertainment-value.

For the sake of entertainment-value the gods "begin" their activity by imagining worlds. Imagining worlds is fun, as can be seen by our experience with forms of fiction: creating films, cartoons, or virtual realities like "Second Life."

Among worlds imagined by gods might be virtual four-dimensional worlds with distinctive beauty and with fictional characters interacting in various ways.

The interaction between the characters in virtual worlds would need to be unpredictable. Fictional stories that have unscripted twists yield more audience-fun than predictable stories.

However, the audience-fun of a mere fictional story is bound to be derivative.

In our fictions the fun is derived from our experiences in real life. We are aware of real life counterparts to the fictional characters. The real life counterparts have real inner lives, and feel the likes of joy and fear. We then imagine, while watching a film or reading a fiction book, that the characters in these narratives have inner lives similar to those of real people or of real animals.

We imagine that being punched hurts our favorite virtual characters. We feel a portion of the grief of the young Lion King who has lost his father. We imagine being another. We empathize.

The gods could have gotten similar entertainment-value from their much more complex invented worlds. They could invent unbelievably detailed virtual worlds. The sheer uniqueness and beauty of each invented world could produce pleasure and satisfaction for gods. Visual art does that for us. The beauty and detail of virtual reality settings has its own value, independently of the story enacted in such settings.

Might the gods have to experience the world from the sensory perspective of the beings in the invented world to fully appreciate the beauty of this invented world? Perhaps so ... as we will see.

Clearly, much of the gods' fun in this fiction exercise would derive from imagining active characters in these virtual worlds. This means that these characters would have to be interesting and multi-dimensional. They could not be lifeless chess pieces, even if such chess pieces moved in unpredictable ways.

Part of the gods' fun, like ours, would derive from imagining that the lives of their favorite characters *matters to* these characters. This means that the gods would have to imagine that the characters possess an aspect of their own reality—the *consciousness* aspect.

The gods would, thus, imagine characters with conscious inner lives.

But now consider this: what if the gods go a step further, beyond merely observing a fictional world and then vicariously imagining themselves as conscious characters of this world?

What if the gods immerse themselves more completely in this imaginative game? What if they imagine themselves as these characters so completely as to forget that they, the gods, are the source of this imaginative immersion?

Would this further imaginative immersion not be more compelling and fun? The answer must be, yes!

But in doing so, would the gods now become *participants*—not just empathetic observers—in this imagined world? It would seem so!

11
Gods, imagined worlds, and participation

Let's recount our fable.

The gods begin by looking for mere fun, so as to enrich their "initial" empty conscious lives.

Then they imagine detailed worlds.

Then they inject unpredictability in the lives of the characters in these worlds.

Then they partially imagine themselves as being these characters—through a vicarious projection of their own inner lives.

Then, they *fully* imagine themselves as these characters, for the sake of more compelling entertainment.

It is undeniably more fun to play an actual part in a story, in a sport, in a role, in a world where wrong choices have consequences, than merely to imagine doing so! Even in fiction, the more completely one forgets oneself and gets caught in the lives of the fictional characters, the more satisfying the fiction-enjoyment is. A *complete* immersion in a fiction world would consist in imaginatively becoming one or more of its characters, leaving behind the perspective of the outside reader or observer or narrator.

Such a complete immersion would be the most complete act of imagination, as well as the most intense and satisfying form of *participation*.

This complete imaginative role-playing, however, turns the fictional characters into ones that consciously do feel and act. The fiction world now becomes a real world, at least for purposes of value and concern!

Ok, we are tempted to suspect that these enlivened fictional characters merely borrow the sense of feeling and acting from a divine immersion in their roles. Perhaps the characters don't really feel and act on their own.

Even if borrowed, however, *an inner life automatically counts*. It is real. If something feels like a pain, like a headache inside a character's head, then it is a pain. If there is an inner sense of being an agent in a story, then for purposes of self-concern there is indeed an agent in this story. Even in a dream-world the terror of being chased by monsters is real terror. The dream-searching for a place to hide has consequences.

If a state feels like a conscious state, and is set in a non-fleeting sequence of such states, in turn set in a non-fleeting virtual world, then it is a conscious state at least as real as a dream state. So we have reached at least the dream-like appearance of an enlivened virtual world.

What we call the real world may simply be a shared, and relatively stable, dream-world.

In any case, once the characters in a dream-like world are consciously enlivened, their well-being counts. That is precisely what makes being a participant in their story and their world compelling, dramatic, and deeply entertaining. A world of many such characters, each equipped with inner lives that matter to each subject, becomes virtually a real world. In fact, such a shared virtual world looks as real as ours!

If we, now, were invented characters in a divine virtual world, our lives would feel exactly as they do now.

Might we, then, be invented characters with borrowed inner lives, living in some divine fiction? Yes, we might be. Nonetheless, *in feeling as though we are real*, in encountering life from a first-person perspective, in being caught in an exciting and precarious life-story, *we have real value*.

A Hamlet, a Scarlet, a Louise, who *felt* anguish and joy and fear of dying would be characters of *real value*, whatever the ultimate fictional-vs.-real status of their world. They deserve to be honored. Even gods might have an obligation to treat them with care.

12
Value is not merely in the eye of the beholder

We have been relying so far on an important assumption: that real value comes at least in part from inner experiences. Is this a safe assumption? Do fictional characters acquire real value as soon as they are equipped with inner lives?

It certainly looks that way. Let's think of objects devoid of inner life. A thoroughly lifeless rock of no special beauty is not a worthy thing, even if it is a unique rock. On the other hand, a rock that pulsates with some inner consciousness is another story. If we knew that a rock is a conscious rock, we would probably give it a name and look for ways to communicate with it. We would not kick it, especially if we believed the rock to be capable of pleasures and pains. Once there is inner life, a rock, or an organism, or a super-organism, becomes endowed with *its own* value.

Since this assumption is so crucial for our tale, we need to investigate it further.

Why think that an inner life magically transforms an ordinary item into something of *intrinsic value*? Isn't value merely in the eye of the observer?

This observer-relative view is popular and tempting, but ultimately we cannot accept it. We certainly cannot accept it regarding everything. We might accept the observer-relative view with regard to chocolate versus vanilla. Which is preferable depends on the taste of the observer. We might accept it with regard to a chipped old cup that belonged to my grandmother. I value it, but there is no reason for others to do so.

But now let's try saying similar things about beings with inner consciousness and feelings:

I value that Jewish child, but there is no reason for you to do so!

I value that Chinese woman, but there is no reason for you to do so!

I value that dog, but there is no reason for you to do so!

I value that human in a coma, but there is no reason for you to do so!

The part about there being no reason for a stranger to value these subjects is problematic. Yes, many groups of humans have believed similar things throughout human history. Yes, we have a natural predisposition to prefer those who are like us. However, we have often seen the horror-filled consequences of such beliefs. At our best we would all reject these claims.

We may wonder if a comatose human has some inner life. However, once we suspect that she does, we no longer imagine that this fleshy object on a bed does not count—even if she is a complete stranger, and we have no attachment to her, and even if she has no family. We begin to worry whether the inner being inside the flesh is comfortable or is in pain; or whether she can hear us.

The anguish of cutting off life-support systems of coma patients is tied to the possible presence of an inner life.

Having an inner life carries a value that is as objective as value can get. Such value would not depend on an outside observer. A lack of external recognition would simply reflect badly on the capacities of the external recognizer.

We simply know from our own case, directly, that an inner life is a thing of wonder! Once present, even the creator of it, even the gods, would have to step back from it and treat it with care—unless gods are sociopathic, or demonic, or totally indifferent.

Presumably genuine gods are neither sociopathic nor demonic. (Naturally, if they were, any attempt to make sense of life would fail).

Totally indifferent gods could have no impulse, no reason, to invent or make any universe.

Real gods, in contrast, would be moved by value, and would consequently have to treat conscious beings with care.

13
The gods must affirm the value of an inner life

Would the gods really have to respect inner value? Let's take a further look at this issue, since many of us are rightly skeptical of impositions of limitations on gods.

Is the intrinsic value of inner lives a constraint on the gods? Aren't gods free to create, invent, affirm, any value they like?

It is true that gods, as super-powerful, should be able to do just about anything. This tempts us to infer that they should be able to turn something into value, or into no value, simply by declaring it so. This is a bad inference, however. It relies on a misunderstanding of what omnipotence is—if there is such a thing.

Omnipotence means being able to do all that can be done. But some things simply cannot be done.

Let's think of analogies. A god can't first make a pyramid-shaped object in our space-time dimensions, and then declare it a cube. Pyramids in our world cannot simultaneously be cubes. Pyramids can be renamed cubes, and vice versa. But these would merely be verbal changes. Verbal changes do not change the nature of the two objects. The one still could not be the other simultaneously. The gods could, of course, make a different world with different structural rules. But that is another story.

Let's apply this analogy to inner value. Can the gods invent a character with some qualitative inner life—with awareness and sentience—and then declare it of no value? The answer must be, no! Inner life is what it is, and it simply has a self-mattering nature. It cares for itself. It wants to go on. It seeks to avoid pain.

In fact, let's turn the question on the gods themselves! Surely if anything counts intrinsically, then genuine gods must so count. Why do they count? What is the basis for of a gods' own value-status, or super-value status? Must the basis not be their inner states?

What else could begin to make the gods sacred, divine, spiritual, exalted, or otherwise highly honored? Their sacredness surely won't derive from their immense or even infinite power. The sun has immense power, yet we do not consider it of sacred worth. Increasing the sun's power to infinity would not change that. That is because we believe the sun to have no *awareness* or *feeling* or *intention*. If we believed otherwise, our judgment would change. Cultures that did believe otherwise did consider the sun to be sacred.

Consider a super cosmic computer full of all the information imaginable, capable of creating and controlling universes, prompted by some internal program, but void of inner conscious life. Would it be a god, or be sacred, or deserve reverence? The answer must be, No. A zombie super-creator is still a zombie.

Even perfect goodness would not be what grants value to a god, *if* the goodness were merely behavioral—consisting of good outward acts with no inner life or intention behind these acts. Even the kindest-behaving of futuristic and organic robots would be no more than a useful tool—if internally lifeless! Increasing the other powers of this robot would not change that. Tools have value, but not intrinsic value.

It is only because we think that a likely divine goodness comes out of genuine intention, and that intention has its home in a field of living awareness, that such goodness begins to gain our respect.

Finally, could a divine living awareness be totally indifferent, even indifferent to itself? No, because a life of complete indifference, even if conceivable, would be paralyzed. It would not produce universes. The presence of at least one universe indicates that a divine life must value something, even if only itself.

If a god valued itself, it could only do so if its own life had self-mattering qualities.

We must conclude that even the value of a divine life is based on the qualities of inner states.

14
Feeling makes value

Have we played the philosophical "why-game" long enough on this matter? Perhaps not. Given the crucial role value plays in our fable, it pays to continue our probe on this topic.

Those less philosophically disposed are free to skip these next three sections.

What is inner life? Why should we think that inner life makes something worthy?

Inner life consists minimally of awareness and feeling (sentience). It is what we lack when we are in a totally dreamless sleep. It is our constant home and companion, so we all recognize it. It is what we are most afraid to lose when we die. The Buddhists have always thought that awareness and feeling (sentience) are the carriers of value, in whatever species of subjects. But, we can ask, why should we agree with them?

It is like something to be a bat, said a famous philosopher. It is not like something to be a rock (presumably). But why does this state of inner being-like-something matter, objectively? Why does having sensations (later we could add emotions, thoughts, dreams, intentions) matter?

We touch on frustratingly basic stuff here.

We want to stay conscious because without consciousness, for us, there might as well be nothing. Without it there might as well be no us. Consciousness is the reason why we each matter, even if only to ourselves. Once present, a conscious being wants to continue being conscious. Consciousness simply matters to itself.

But why? It is difficult to say why. Part of the answer is that it feels like something to be oneself, to be a human, to be a cat. Part of the answer must be that a conscious life matters because it carries with it desirable and undesirable qualities, like pleasures and pains. Why are these desirable or undesirable? They are desirable or undesirable, from the inside, because it is the nature of pleasures to please, and of pains to hurt. They are desirable or undesirable simply because of their nature.

Let's look at bodily pains. When we feel toothaches we all rush for pain-relief pills. We do so to avoid the pains. They must be bad things if we want to avoid them! What makes pains bad?

They are bad things because of the sheer nature of the ache-feelings! Here we probably reach the final link in the chain of explanation.

One can keep insisting that this is no proof that a toothache is bad. But this is merely academic, as the expression goes! One's behavior, when one's teeth ache, will belie this skeptical insistence.

One might think, however, that a toothache is only bad for the agent with the bad tooth? Why would it count as bad from another's perspective? Can't one hold a view that only one's own pains are bad?

The following is one way of testing these agent-relative claims.

Let's say my migraine is a bad thing for me. Let's now ask this: is my migraine bad because it is *my* migraine, or is it bad because it is an *ache*? Surely, we must take the second option. Each of a pair of Siamese twins, even when unsure whose migraine each is feeling, would beg for pain-relief pills. Each of them would not care that the feeling might be the other's ache. Each would simply want the pain stopped.

Besides, let's not forget that thoughts and pleasures can be as much *mine* as my migraines, without thoughts and pleasures being thereby bad. In fact my pleasures are rather good. Being mine, thus, is not the source of the negative value of my pains.

Pains are bad because they hurt.

15
Feeling makes value. Part two

Bodily pain is *itself* bad, and bodily pleasure is *itself* good? Let's try another well-known imaginative test.

Imagine you are captured by value-testing scientists. They force you to push one or two buttons, before they let you go. One button will produce 5 minutes of intense migraine for some creature at some corner of a far away galaxy—not necessarily a human creature. The second button will cause 5 minutes of intense pleasure, like a warm bath on a shivering body, or like listening to one's favorite music, for a similarly distant creature. Which do you press?

If that is all you know, and you also know what pain is, then you have strong and non-personal reasons not to press the pain button. How could you wish pain on anyone?

It is no surprise that we cannot bear to see the pain of our spouse, our dog, our cat. It is no surprise that most soldiers that injure and kill come back home with deep psychological scars.

Ok, we may occasionally wish to inflict pain on scoundrels as punishment. But this is further indication that pain, if it is to be a punishment, must be a bad thing! We don't want the scoundrel to be repaid with something neutral or with something good. We want to inflict something bad on the scoundrel.

Will the preceding button-pressing experiment persuade an observer devoid of compassion? Will it persuade a sadist? The answer, of course, is No.

However, let's not make too much of this. What is objective or real is not necessarily recognizable by everyone.

Colors are real. There is a real difference between red and green. Yet blind persons may fail to recognize this difference. Or if they can, by means of some wavelength-recognizing machine, they will do so in a manner completely different from the way we do. They might capture a distinction with the right equipment, but it will be a non-visual distinction—perhaps they will capture a neutral wavelength-frequency distinction! They would still not know what green and red look like. They would still not see the beauty of roses. The incapacity on the part of some to recognize our normal red and green does not call into question the reality of these colors.

Similar things can be said for sound and music. That some cannot hear music the way we can does not make music unreal. Nor is music merely a pattern of air-waves.

Some humans and many animals that can't see colors or hear music simply miss out on important dimensions of our world. We ourselves may miss out on other important dimensions. All of us only see a small section of the electromagnetic spectrum. Deer can see farther into the ultraviolet spectrum than humans.

This need for recognition capacities can even apply to the solidity of rocks. A being equipped only with powerful microscopic vision, and no sense of touch, would not separate rocks from rivers. Such a being would only see fields of molecules or of ever smaller components like atoms or electrons. Solidity would disappear. All would be seen as vibrating, fast moving stuff. Yet rocks are quite different from rivers.

The real features that define our world need appropriate recognition capacities. This applies to colors, music, rocks, and sensation-value. There may be some naked reality at bottom, but for "it" to be apprehended, to be known, it must be apprehended as something of some definite kind. And "it" must be apprehended through some definite sensory or other recognition-capacity.

The real is complex. It needs both stuff "out there" and the right perceiver. This applies to the reality of pain and value. A person of no compassion may lack the capacity to fully appreciate the nature of pain. Such a person may recognize pains in the way that a blind person recognizes the color green—through some instrument, but coldly. The sadist may have an even more warped recognition power in this area.

Neither the indifferent nor the sadist will then be persuaded of the badness of pain.

16
Feeling makes value. Part three

Pain is *itself* bad, and pleasure is *itself* good? Let's give skepticism one final shot.

Isn't there something paradoxical about saying that some *subjective* states of an agent, like pleasure and pain, matter intrinsically? For if they matter in their own right, and then they would matter directly and independently of the judgments of observers. This would mean that they must matter *objectively*?

How can subjective states matter objectively?

There is no real paradox here. Subjective states need a subject, by their very nature. But that fact should not be confused with dependence on observers.

Let's keep in mind that subjective states are weird, but they are also real. They belong among the real furniture of the universe. The experience of pain is as undeniably there, present, real, as are planets and atoms. Only the mistake of thinking that what is real is the external, or that which can be measured by our physical instruments, hides this fact.

Pains, dreams, love, fantasies, clearly exist, even while they are not directly accessible from the outside. Brain states that correlate with these experiences can be externally accessed. However, brain neural correlates are very different things from pain or dream experiences, much to the dismay of many current philosophers and scientists. Neural correlates are neither private nor show weird internal content.

Consciousness itself, that without which nothing else would seem to matter, is only accessible from the inside. Yet it as immediately real, to those who have it, as anything can be. Only the habit of thinking of the real as that which has external object-like status bars us from seeing this most obvious of facts. (Let's recall, also, that having some distinct object-like status may also require a conscious perceiver).

Let's recall, also, that if there ever was a god "before" all physical worlds, there would have been simply a divine massive subjectivity.

What else can a god, as a powerful mind, be? This massive subjectivity would have been the only objective reality. Thus, there is no necessary clash between inner reality and its status as real or objective.

It follows that if some subjective states like pleasure and pain carry a kind of self-mattering—in that they matter by means of how they feel— then *they simply matter*.

If they self-matter, then they indeed matter objectively.

It is no surprise that we worry about the inner life of comatose patients. Are they aware, and are they comfortable?

It is no surprise that more and more people worry about the inner lives of cats, cows, and possibly plants. If they feel, can we kill them for fun or for food?

It is no surprise that at some point we'll ask of intelligent robots: "Is there really some feeling behind that look and behind those words?"

This appeal to sentience, or to consciousness and feeling, as one basis of intrinsic value does not rule out the fact that bad experiences are sometimes useful for good ends. Even toothaches can serve good ends. They can warn us of tooth decay.

This useful role, however, does not take away their badness. It is precisely their awful aching quality—their badness—that shakes us into action. We want to stop these awful sensations

It is also worth noting that even if we are convinced that sentience has intrinsic and objective value, it would not have to be the only basis for value. We have already alluded to beauty as another type of value. As we will see, it is likely that there are other ones, and perhaps even higher types of values.

Finally, let's note that if the real values of color and pleasure experiences are only accessible from the inside, then a god intent on accessing such values would have to take up our point of view and our sensory-recognition capacities.

A god would have to play at being us.

17
Can we really imagine god-beings?

After this necessary philosophical parenthesis, concerning intrinsic value, let's return to our main fable.

We began with divine sources, whose intentions, we claimed, must aim at value and at enhanced inner lives. Neither divine arbitrariness nor indifference is a real option.

Can we really speak intelligibly about such super-beings? If not, what we have done so far is nonsense.

This challenge leads, unfortunately, to the need for another philosophical parenthesis.

Many have claimed that our minds cannot imagine or conceive a genuine god. Some have backed these claims by pointing to a god's alleged otherness, or total ineffability, or total transcendence.

We must reject these pessimistic claims. These are, at best, overstatements. At worst, they are claims used to mystify, and to offer cover for all sorts of nonsense. Let's keep in mind that behind this seeming intellectual modesty—"we can't know!"—there is not mere silence, as one would expect. There are, instead, many books and many sets of "divine" teachings (which we are often told to accept blindly).

Let's put modesty aside. We can indeed *partially* imagine a god. We have just seen that an inner life must be present in some being for it to be more than a sun or a good-producing cosmic robot. *A god must be or have a consciousness.*

We also reasoned that in order for this world not to be some uncontrolled divine accident there must be some divine motive behind it. *A god-being, therefore, must have intention-like capacities.*

We have seen that divine conscious intentions cannot be arbitrary. That means that *divine intentions must aim at value.*

These features give us significant information about divine beings.

Sure, we must avoid silly humanizations. A god will not be a 4-limbed or 8-limbed being. It will not live on a throne in the clouds. It does not have a booming voice, or an eye that looks at four directions. It does not speak Hebrew, English, or Chinese. It does not have spouses or children. Yes, a son of god is a silly notion, whether it is Christian or Hindu. A "jealous" god is also a silly notion. There is a long list of these.

On the other hand, we can also go too far in the impersonal direction, toward Dao-like notions. A god is unlikely to be some serene, timeless, semi-frozen inner being, free of impulses, motives, thought-contents. This would border on attributing to a god a form of listlessness and lifelessness.

Such a serene and timeless god brings to mind the permanent and changeless world of platonic forms. Even if perfect, such forms resemble too closely a frozen world. The agency element is lacking.

Suppose we added a state of unchanging bliss to an impersonal Dao: would that suffice to make it more alive? Perhaps. Still, such a being remains ... dull and passive. Related visions of paradise, according to which we remain forever in the blissful unchanging presence of god, may have some appeal—but mainly for those of us who are weary and are looking for peace. Most of us want more than unchanging eternal peace. We also want more than mindless adoration. We probably want more than a merging in an eternal and impersonal divine bliss, like a nirvana.

In our current state we certainly want new music and new adventures! We want to know what happens to the ones we left behind! We want to know what happens to our favorite movement, nation, planet, sports-team! If eventually we lose interest in these favorites, we will probably seek others.

In our current state, we care about the newness of the next day. Stories, adventures, and twists engage us. Most importantly, being the active protagonist of our own story engages us. These are current human longings. Are they merely current ones? Are they merely human ones?

18
Gods, longings, and action

Let's continue to play the game of being gods.

We can be pretty sure that gods must be conscious and intentional beings. Must they also have longings for the new and the adventuresome, in ways analogous to our longings?

Imagine being a god, a being ensconced in utter safety and in unchanging contentment or even bliss. Imagine that nothing changes for this god, not now, not ever. There is inner intense contentment eternally!

Is such a life the best that a god can do? Probably not, though we are in perilous territory here.

Can we argue that if such a life does not even satisfy a human, it cannot possibly satisfy a god?

Let's consider this: what would this god have to be content or blissful about? If nothing, then this bliss would not differ in kind from an objectless and endless narcotic high. Ok, it would be a super, super-high. It would be a divine high. Still, can any immense super-high or a bliss-state be *content-free and yet noble*?

How dare we, mere mortals, say no? And yet we must. A state of bliss, for no reason and with no content, is unworthy of a god.

Compare our narcotic highs to highs tied to accomplishments— like a runner's high for instance; or the high of a team victory, of a poem-creation, of saving a life. Why are we proud of the latter highs, but not of the former? It clearly is because they have some content that is tied to agency and accomplishments.

Wouldn't divine highs also have to be of this nobler kind? A god who is wrapped in a permanent objectless high is unworthy of respect. We might envy such a being in some ways, since we all like feeling happy even if for no reason. That is what some drugs are for. But envy and respect are separate things.

If a self-absorbed, merely blissful god is not a noble god, what is the alternative? The alternative is a god who is also active in some sense, and whose satisfactions or bliss reflect some value-related activity. Perhaps this activity is some form of free self-formation and self-expansion. Perhaps a god must be an unfinished being, perpetually engaged in reaching new heights.

It might help to remember that there are different forms of perfection. Different perfections are appropriate for different things. There is the perfect circle, the perfect baseball game, and maybe even the perfect life. Finally, there is perfect living. Only this last requires ongoing aliveness.

Perfect living may require more than unchanging bliss. Perhaps the highest form of living perfection, as opposed to lifeless kinds, requires ever higher forms of accomplishment or growth or expansion or improvement. This highest form of perfection may require ongoing agency.

To be fully complete, perfectly finished, is to be either passive or dead. Perfect Platonic Forms, like the standard of beauty or the perfect circle, would be like that. They are perfect standards, but not alive. A finished life, even if perfect, is a dead life. A perfect baseball game is a finished one.

A life of permanent and endless bliss may not be a dead life, but there is dullness to it. An ongoing life, properly enriched, surely is preferable to a completed life, even if this latter is in other senses perfect. To be fully alive, in whatever form, is to be engaged in ongoing longings. Among longings, the noble ones aspire to things that matter, and have not yet been attained. They aspire to new realms, or higher realms. Perhaps ongoing longings for things of value will require endless higher realms.

We will see, through a well-known test, that a life of passive blissfulness, even when papered over by the mere appearance of activity, is not as desirable as one of genuine activity. The active life generally trumps the blissful life. Thus, the longing for the new and the adventuresome may not be confineable to us. An active god might also long for its own higher forms of the new and the adventuresome.

19
The life of an active god

We have argued that a divine life is an active life. An inactive life of permanent bliss borders too closely on dullness. It suffers from a deep metaphysical incompleteness. The agency side a life adds a crucial element to mere feeling. Even the highest form of feeling—content-free bliss—is not enough. Doings add to life. Doings also bring with them the new and unexpected.

What kind of activity might be appropriate for a god? As always, we continue our game by starting from what we know.

Our active lives are ones driven by various aspirations. We naturally want to ensure safety and at least minimal comfort. These aspirations, we said, are not applicable to gods.

Besides safety and comfort, we yearn for fun, for the new, for the surprising—and for the beautiful and the great. Our aspirations are linked to value. They are not random. We long to hear a new Dylan song, like "Things Have Changed." We don't long to hear traffic noise.

We must imagine that divine activity is also linked to aspirations that are not random, and that are tied to value. There is no reason why some of this value should not be linked to new experiences, new adventures, new fun, and new beauty. Why should the ecstasy of music, of games, of spring flowers, be reserved only for lesser beings like us?

True, there are some good things, like pain-relief, that come from flawed states, such as being in pain. Since gods lack flawed states, they would also neither need nor want the correlated relief-goods. However, other good things don't seem to require prior flawed states. Adventure, play, music, and flowers are among these.

As the Hindu theologian Shankara put it, a self-sufficient super royalty does not merely bask in its self-sufficient safety and contentment. He or she would not merely want to freeze time forever, so as to maintain this state of good fortune. At minimum, this super royalty will seek to play games, read books, travel, and follow the ups and downs of its family or subjects. A background condition of safety and contentment is certainly desirable. However, with that assured, one wants more. One wants that new song, or that new movie, or the coming of another spring!

It is true, as Buddhists remind us, that that new song and new spring will not satisfy us permanently. It is true that we will want still newer songs and seasons. It does not follow that wanting itself is a problem. Permanent satisfaction may be the problem. Permanent satisfaction perhaps can only be attained though some form of bliss-value. But not all value is bliss-value. Wanting may be the stuff of life and of nobility.

Yes, a god's inner state surely transcends the inner state of even our mightiest human kings and queens.

This, however, only shows that divine sorts of wants and accomplishments will include ones that are unimaginably higher than human ones. Divine accomplishments might be in the order of imagining and inventing universes *ex-nihilo*. They will include inventing new existence frameworks, like space-time.

These magnificent inventions would still be dynamic accomplishments. They would be expressions of some agency.

For instance, divine doings could pay off in infinite ways. Even a high-level divine existence could be enriched a little through the unexpected ecstasy of our own music and of our games and of the color and smells of our spring flowers.

True, a divine consciousness is not attached to a body with eyes and ears that sense the color of spring roses and the music of Dylan or Bach. But the gods do have us. We can be their eyes and ears. The divine game of part-taking in human and non-human forms is likely to be tied to such unique joys.

Value-enrichment is, after all, the goal!

20
The gods as temporal beings

We noted that a changeless platonic perfect state resembles too closely a frozen world. Genuine living gods must be active and must aspire to value.

Must the gods then, particularly if active, live in a temporal setting? Our tale talks of gods seeking enrichment and then inventing and then participating in worlds. This manner of speaking uses ideas of beginning and subsequent states. Must gods live in time?

This has obviously been hotly debated. Many theologians and mystics have claimed that the inner life of a super-god must lie outside of time—it must be timeless.

Yet it appears that any inner life, to be fully alive, must stir with awareness, and must require some internal dynamism. A consciousness that experiences no change, no humming, no vibration, no flow, seems frozen or empty. How would it even differ from non-consciousness?

Some internal dynamism may have to be essential to consciousness. This dynamism is even more essential if a divine consciousness is to display agency.

Perhaps a divine internal dynamism is of an alien type, and different from our temporal one. Mystics do speak of some non-temporal but also non-frozen present—a spacious present. Might the gods reside in this kind of dynamic spacious present?

This is a difficult issue. Non-temporal life-forms are especially puzzling for us.

What remains clear is that a divine inner life that is static and changeless, or that is merely self-absorbed in a permanent bliss, cannot explain the non-static impulse to produce (or become, or dream, or imagine) our temporal world.

A changeless life, even if possible, cannot yield new fruits like this universe.

If a temporal world unfolded from some pre-temporal phase, something must have occurred inside a god that led to this temporal world. Some dynamism—either a temporal or a super-temporal one—appears necessary in a god-being to explain the presence of our reality. We are tempted to think, here, of a god as having existed before the world, perhaps even before time itself. Our image is that a pre-time god imagines or creates our world. Since this imagined or created world is framed by space-time, time begins at this point.

But we have to be careful of such temptations. Perhaps, in our terms, there was never a divine state "before" time.

Suppose we try to think of a divine state before time. Could a god at no-time create or imagine a time-beginning? If it imagined a time-beginning "before" there was time, god's no-time state becomes a kind of pre-first-moment-state. Pre-first-moments look a lot like additional time phases.

This cannot be, since the god who imagines time is supposed to be in no-time.

Are we stuck in paradox here?

21
Imagining a god and its temporal element.
Part two

Let's see if we can escape time paradoxes here. We are trying to understand how a timeless god can actively come to imagine or create a temporal world.

Let's try a different thought.

Perhaps a god imagines at once an entire world with all of its infinitely long time-expanse, including what we call the future. On this conception, god does not just imagine the first moment-state of a world, but all the moments. God's "original" state would then be equidistant from each and every moment of time.

This in turn would mean that the current moment of time is as close to the "original" divine imagining or creation as was some moment 15 billions of years ago (one scientific estimate of the "beginning" of our universe). We could then say that our world, from a god's perspective, "begins" as much now as 15 billion years ago, or 15 billion years in our future.

Continuing this conception, we might say that a god might not have to face this spatio-temporal world on a before-after basis, unlike us. A god might face our temporal world as if facing many simultaneous now-moments. These simultaneous now-moments could be the spacious present of the mystics, or Tillich's eternal now. The future would be a now to a God. Its creation, or imagining, would be a "continuous" one, and not a once-upon-a-time happening.

Can a god really face our space-time world in this timeless fashion?

Two related factors have to be kept in mind before we can say yes: genuine free will, and the surprise factor.

The picture of a divine perspective that sees all world-moments as now-moments reminds us of a similar picture. This is the picture of the successive frames of an old tape-movie that are unrolled flat on a table. These successive frames would be equally and simultaneously present to us.

Such pictures call into question our free will. Many theologians have worried about this.

If god knows in a now-sense all our future outcomes, how can genuine alternatives really be available to us at any choice-moment?

More importantly, we have seen that part of the value-reason for worlds, from god's entertainment perspective, is the element of adventure and surprise. If the entire world, including the future, is present simultaneously to a god, then there would be no sense of adventure and surprise. A god that knows all the outcomes will not be surprised!

How do we simultaneously hold together a non-temporal god, a surprise-filled virtual world, and characters with genuine free will?

22
Imagining a god and its temporal element.
Part three

We want to combine a non-temporal god, a surprise-filled virtual world, and characters with genuine free will.

A resolution is possible. A god might operate on more than one level of awareness.

As we saw before, a god will seek to pour itself fully into its imaginings, partly so as to attain thrill-values.

Pouring itself fully into its imaginings requires some relinquishing of its greater nature and powers. Such relinquishing of its greater nature and powers might include a god's leaving behind its no-time or super-temporal perspective, even if a god had such a perspective.

We asked whether a god can really face our space-time world in a timeless fashion. The answer might be: Yes, but that for reasons of participation a god might opt not do so. Imagine a motherly queen who has the power to watch the simultaneous goings-on of the crowds in the villages below while perched on a high castle, but chooses to mingle with the crowds instead. A god might have the super-temporal power to see all temporal moments simultaneously, but could similarly choose to participate in that temporal world.

Alternatively, a god is surely capable of operating on many levels of awareness. We have already imagined that, in becoming us, a god would adopt countless individual temporal perspectives. If a god's viewpoint can splinter into countless simultaneous first-person perspectives, it also might be able to retain the queenly above-it-all super-temporal perspective. Like a coin with two sides, a god might display a splintered temporal side, and a unified non-temporal one.

Clearly, a full divine participation in worlds that we have been envisaging needs a suspension of a god's extra-temporal perspective. In fact, a *fully participatory god* would also have to suspend its awareness of other imagined worlds, and even of its other individualized first-person perspectives. To participate in the human perspective a god cannot take the role of generic humanity. A god would have to take the role of specific actual humans, like you or Tom Lapic.

To derive thrill-value from an imagined world like ours, a god must be caught in the roles of the imagined and living characters. A god cannot face this world as an outside audience, timeless or otherwise. An outside observer only derives mild thrill-value.

In being caught in the thrills of adventure and surprise *through* the experiences and decisions and adventures of the characters, a god must be caught in space-time. To be so caught, some self-imposed partial forgetfulness of its higher powers is necessary.

Naturally, not all of a divine awareness can get so caught. First, this is because if it were, then the captivity might be permanent and inescapable—a god would have lost its background sense of safety. Second, a god's energy might be inexhaustible. If so, it would not be exhausted even by its countless roles in imagined worlds. The divine potential and possibilities might be such as to always aspire beyond the realized possibilities.

This transcendence of the real, of the currently realized, might take many forms, some of which we might not understand. But this transcendence of the real might also take the form of a perpetual yearning for the new and the different on the part of the conscious agents in these worlds.

This transcendence of the real might even take the form of an embedded sense, within the conscious agents in these worlds, that there is more to reality than the stuff and the perspectives of that particular world.

Perhaps because of this basic urge for something greater the more self-conscious characters in all worlds, including most humans, will feel as if they are of that world but *not only* of that world.

Many of us have such a sense. This sense might be a sign that we are indeed characters powered by an inexhaustible divine imagination.

23
A god needs worlds

We have been imagining the fable of a god that enhances its thrill-values by turning itself into separate inner lives, separate minds, placed in various worlds. In doing so, a god would have to leave behind its other perspectives, including super-temporal ones.

Might there be additional and even deeper reasons for a god to play this game of participation and of self-forgetting? Perhaps there are.

In general, an inner life, a center of consciousness, appears to need a medium or setting in which to exist meaningfully.

This is at least true for our inner lives.

In our case, we see objects and light and colors, located in a framework of space; and their changes are experienced in a framework of time. We see through eyes. Eyes are a sensory mechanism attached to a body, itself an object in space-time. We also feel warmth, we taste foods, and we experience movement. We do movements. We are embodied, in a world of bodily forms spread out in space-time media.

What about a divine mind? What would a pure, pre-worlds, divine mind experience? What would a free-floating powerful nowhere-consciousness experience?

Let's try to imagine a pure divine mind, one that does not see or touch or sense movement or feel cold. It would have no body or senses. It would not see colors. It would not be in a setting, like time-space.

Could it experience without experiencing something defined by such a setting? What would it think about? Could it even have definite thought-contents without experiencing something well-defined?

This reminds us of the point that naked reality can only be apprehended from some perspective or other. Pure energy, pure stuff, in no form remains no more than pure potential. Any actual reality needs form.

Perhaps the "original" state of a god is just one infinite potential, seeking form.

Suppose an original divine mind were only to think about itself—an Aristotelian god. What would it think? Without thinking of itself in some form, a god's thoughts and imaginings about itself would be ... what? Empty powerful vibrations ... though inward and alive? I Am what I Am? Is this even a thought?

Can the I-perspective have any meaning in a state of pure potentiality? Even the thought "I am a god" might have no meaning in the absence of self-form and of contrasting other-forms. "I am a god" must at least imply "I am not a tree, a house, a physical universe..."

We are risking here, in trying to imagine the deepest things.

Yet we must imagine that even if a god were to think only of itself, this god might have to imagine itself in some form or other, and as belonging to some world or other.

To be inward and alive, while not feeling warm or cold, tired or fresh, or anything specific ... might be to have a yearning for ... something not yet specified or available. This yearning might turn out to be the longing for definite forms of being and for forms of expression.

Thus, the very essence of a god, the conscious core of an immense divine consciousness, might be linked to imagining itself being something or other, or many things or other.

Not to imagine itself as something or other might be, for a super-consciousness, to remain a mere indefinite potential.

A god will, then, seek actualities. Hence, a god will form worlds.

24
A god needs worlds. Part two

We are still exploring the nature of a god, while continuing our fable of gods becoming universes.

We risked the claim that the very essence of a god is linked to imagining itself being something or other. Not to do so, for a pure super-consciousness, is to remain a powerful but indefinite conscious energy potential.

We claimed that even thought-contents need to derive from some contact—even if merely imaginative—with some definite world.

Let's consider the example of intentions, since we have to attribute intentions to a god that produces worlds like ours.

Could a divine free-floating nowhere-mind, in no-place and in no-time, even *have* intentions?

Intentions must not only take place (we would say "happen"), but they also must aim, and they must aim at some content. This content might be merely imagined. One can intend to produce a purely fictional world. Nonetheless, one cannot imagine this fiction without imagining it as having some definite form.

The imagined something must differ from other things imaginable. To imagine a triangle is not to imagine a circle. Form and definition imply dimensions and borders. Dimensions and borders constitute, or rely on, the framework of a world.

Thus, a god that intends is a god that imagines specific worlds.

No matter how powerful and divine, *a god with an inner life of thought, intention, and imagination, is a god that imagines one or more worlds.*

Of course, a god-mind is unlikely to limit its self-imagining to that of a being in a time-space world. This world-form would be only one imaginable world. Still, a god might need to keep imagining itself in world-forms.

We could even dare to suggest that imagining worlds is the primary divine activity. Imagining worlds might be a vehicle for divine thought-contents and divine self-awareness. It might be the means of a meaningful divine life. Imagining worlds might be the means for a god's psychological expansion or improvement!

Let's also recall, in this context, that world-imaginings are needed for a god-mind to express its longing for value. We saw that without such longing, and the satisfactions linked to value, a god's actions would be arbitrary or even non-existent. There must be some value in self-awareness, self-definition, and self-knowledge, or else why seek it.

Our own longing for value prompts us to make music, or to improve our tennis game, or to share our knowledge, or to help others. A similar longing would prompt a god to imagine worlds, and thereby to enhance value through its participation in the imagined worlds.

Participation in these worlds would, in turn, yield unique new values: like music and tennis games.

The Hindu myth of a divine Brahman that opts to turn itself into many different beings and worlds is a rich myth indeed.

25
More divine imaginings: variety

So, our fable tells of a god or gods with inner lives and intentions, imagining worlds, and aiming at value.

Value is most directly tied to inner lives. The experience of colors and sounds adds value. Thus, a god's impulse toward value would prompt a move toward worlds with new types of inner lives – perhaps an infinite variety of such consciousnesses. Having many duplicates of one type of consciousness is less fun and less compelling than having many types.

Each new type of consciousness and each new individual could help enhance value partly through unique perspectives and experiences.

Worlds and environments, whether imaginary or real, need to unfold as settings for meaningful conscious lives. New realities would have to emerge into form to house conscious lives.

From our vantage point of an already emerged, formed, externalized world, we might interpret the "original" emergence as a temporal big-bang.

The sheer existence of new inner lives—ones that will yield new experiences as they encounter and interact with new unfolding environments—would automatically carry value. Felt color and sound carry value. So does the experience of moving in space-time, up a hill, on a cool morning. These unique experiences, by themselves, are sufficient purposes for worlds.

Imagine an initial divine state of infinite pure potentiality. Then imagine an actual "later" experience of an embodied definite individual climbing a sunny hill. That pure divine potentiality has been enriched in a small unique way. Once there is an imagined actual world, the presence of a vast variety of inner lives elevates the value of this world. The urge to expand value would explain the presence of radically different conscious forms.

The inner lives of different humans will vary, and often vary significantly. Yet, most will experience colors, sounds, and the taste of garlic in much the same way.

The need for variety would call for other and different sensory ways of encountering earth's reality.

This helps to explain the presence of radically different inner lives on our planet, such as those of bats, dolphins, frogs, alligators, wasps, and a million others.

There may, of course, be life-forms that are even more alien compared to those we recognize. Perhaps these alien life-forms inhabit non-earth-like settings and are based on unknown senses.

For all we know, there are worlds not built around "external" frameworks like that of space-time-matter. We must not be too parochial in imagining possible life forms.

26
More divine imaginings: surprise

So, our fable has gods that aim at value. Value is tied to inner lives. Uniqueness and variety add value. Thus, a god will imagine many varieties of inner lives to maximize inner-lives value.

We have already noted that a second value-element behind the emergence of worlds is the element of *surprise*.

In order for new life-forms in new worlds to be more than mere centers of feeling—varied, worthy, but passive—they need the agency element. These life forms must have impulses. Agency and impulses open the way for unpredictability, adventure, and surprise.

Agency, adventure, and surprise further enrich the inner lives of the participants—the divine imaginative characters who have now become agents themselves—by making use of the element of the unknown. Unknowable futures enhance the felt preciousness of a present life.

This thrill and surprise felt by agents will also serve to simultaneously add objective value to the imagined universe. We have seen that a rich inner life carries both entertainment value and objective value.

To make the adventure doubly entertaining, the unpredictability must come partly from outside events, but also from inside. Each spark of new life-forms must be endowed with impulses and with the mysterious power of free will. This last is the sheer primitive power to choose this way or that way—at least with respect to options perceived as viable by the agent. We often face such options in contexts of competing and undecided impulses.

The free will power is the ultimate surprise-producing factor. As ultimate, not even the gods can predict its outcomes. As ultimate, it adds a strange sort of control and thrill for the agent, and indirectly for the divine creative force behind the agent. This divine force would derive indirect thrills in the way a parent derives pleasure from the child's independent choices and accomplishments.

Whether some level of free will must be part and parcel of any consciousness, including less complex forms, we can only guess. Our best guess is, Yes. But we cannot be sure.

We can also not be sure how far down consciousness reaches. Are plants and cells conscious? Are molecules? Does consciousness, of varied levels of complexity, pervade everything? Are all levels of consciousness involved in minimal choice-making?

What matters here is that the new centers of consciousnesses that lend value to newly imagined world-settings will be *active*. They will explore, figure new things out, look for new experiences. In more advanced cases they will invent tools and form new partnerships and organizations.

These centers of consciousnesses will seek natural pleasure, love, and beauty. They will seek these in many new forms. They will imagine ever newer forms of pleasure, love, and beauty. They will produce unforeseeable new values—music, poetry, cathedrals, books, films, ski-lifts, planes, and pizza.

Those centers of consciousnesses that can step away from their own inner lives, the ones capable of advanced self-consciousness, will try to understand themselves and this new world. They will also want to know how their lives are connected to ultimate purposes.

In inheriting the inner impulses of the gods, including curiosity and value impulses, these new agents will forever seek the new and the different and the better.

27
A first summary: we are here because we enhance value

We have come to a first summary-take of the moral of our fable: answering why we and the world are here. *We are here because we enhance cosmic and ultimate value.*

We have noted that a god-being must have an inner life and some intention-like capacities. For it not to be demonic, it must at least eschew anti-value intentions. For it not to be arbitrary, it must aim at value.

We have tried to show that fundamental value resides at least in part in self-mattering states, and that these are linked to inner lives. We noted also that our cosmos includes these value-parts—*namely, beings with conscious lives that care.* Some such beings are like us, and others are unlike us.

It is not much of a stretch to conclude that the presence in our world of beings with qualitative inner lives is linked intimately to divine intentions that aim at enhancing value.

We are here because we matter, and the gods want to enrich their lives by producing things that matter—by producing beings with living points of view!

What else can we infer?

A god's impulse toward value would prompt an imaginative move toward new and varied types of inner lives and correlated worlds. New inner lives enhance value through unique spectrums of feelings, and through unique choices and actions. A god intent on deriving the most satisfaction out of these new lives is one that pours itself and participates in such lives.

Any unique awareness—combined with unique impulses, choices, and actions—requires encountering a world from a felt individual center. In our case, this is a body with sensory capacities that reveal to us a unique sense of outside. The "inside" we feel and think. The "outside" we experience as our own body in a world of other bodies, interacting within a space-time four-dimensional board.

Interaction within this four-dimensional medium is not merely the stuff of physics—bodies affecting bodies. The *felt* par t is the value-crucial part. Our felt embodiment makes possible the unique taste of apples and of pizza, the exhilaration of climbing mountains or of playing in soccer games or of engaging in dizzying sexual encounters. Each of these adds a unique value to both our lives and to the universe.

A divine mind looking to multiply value would, thus, imagine itself in limited body-forms with particular senses. It might imagine itself in countless varieties of physical forms. It would do so to experience countless unique things: among these, the taste of apples and of pizza, the smell of roses, the thrill of tennis-playing, and the intoxicating experience of sniffing catnip for cats!

This gives us one answer to the big questions: why are we here at all, and why are we in this form? Our existence is value-explained.

Our unique experiences carry value, because all forms of positive-quality experience carry value, and because our forms are sui generis—unlike any others. Nothing tastes quite like beer or garlic! No taste of beer and of garlic can be experienced unless one has our unique physical and sensory forms.

Since the gods seek experiential enrichment, they will seek varieties of unique values. In doing so, they will also seek to imagine being us.

Indeed, they will seek to *be* us.

28
We are here because we enhance value. Part two

We are continuing the initial summary of the moral of our fable.

We have seen that since the gods must seek value, they will seek to feel *our* unique experiences, among others. They will then imagine being us. To do so *fully* is equivalent to being us.

We have seen that values linked with *activity* must be added to the values linked with unique *felt experiences*.

A god would seek more than the unique taste of ripe figs and the unique smell of roses. A god would want to experience the drama factor involved in perilous undertakings. This explains why we are not only passive sensing beings, but active characters engaged in ongoing and open-ended stories.

Being so engaged adds a cluster of new values, like thrill, suspense, overcoming, and hope. The dramatic part is linked to the possibility of failure, injury, loss, death—our own and those of others.

Each role and perilous life is also unique. Each of us springs from a different and immensely complex set of psychological settings, and from different social circumstances and challenges.

We may be tiny creatures in a vast universe, but each of our lives is immensely rich. Only great novels come close to capturing the detailed richness of one day of a person's inner life. James' Joyce's *Ulysses* comes to mind. Since this rich inner lived drama is at least part of what matters, we each matter. Each of our unique lived adventures adds value to the universe.

This is not true only of humans. But it is especially true of humans.

Our active aspect, the aspect tied to our story and adventure, paves the way for new and unique accomplishments.

It is true that we don't have to prove ourselves or accomplish great goals in order to carry worth. Accomplishments, however, are more than mere icings on the cake.

The creation and experience of music, of paintings, of cathedrals, of novels, films, and civilizations, these are part of the new and unpredictable creative surprises unleashed by the gods. They did not imagine themselves being us for nothing, or only for the sake of unique natural sensations and feelings!

The gods must have seen that they could do better.

They imagined themselves as life-forms equipped with their own mini-imaginative powers, and placed in settings that permit these mini-imaginative powers to create and appreciate unique new values.

Many of these unique new values created would have been absolutely unforeseeable in the "initial" imagining of our world. No god could have foreseen a Saint Peter's Basilica, a Michelangelo painting in the Sistine Chapel, a Christian system of thought, a *Moby Dick*!

They might have known that each new world is fecund and brimming with possibilities, certain to yield unique fruits. However, no one could have known which fruits a world imbued with freedom will yield.

This all adds up. A mature divine being would imagine free and active centers of consciousness, who in turn imagine and outwardly realize unique items of greatness—and, also, of horror.

The horror part we will have to address later.

29
The value of products

Our fable has put a lot of weight on experiential values. These are the ones that self-matter. What about other sorts of value? What about the just-mentioned values tied to human great accomplishments and products?

When looking at great accomplishments we face two value-challenges. Both challenges aim to reduce all value to feeling-value or experiential value.

We claimed that things like music, paintings, cathedrals, novels, films, civilizations, and so forth, add an additional sort of value to the value of inner felt experiences. Might the value of such great products derive merely from the satisfactions they prompt in observers? Might this value be reducible to experiential value—like that of my grandmother's broken cup that means something to me, but has no intrinsic value? Might great music simply mean something to us, without having its own intrinsic value?

The second related question is this: might the value of our actual accomplishment derive *only* from the subjective satisfactions we feel in the course of producing these accomplishments?

Philosophers have, of course, long debated whether all value might reduce to feeling-value. Reductionist answers are always tempting because they make our understanding of the world easier. Yet, as with physicalist reductionism (all that exists is physical), we should be weary of a reductionist answer here (all that counts is feeling).

Let's take the first question. Might our great works count as great *merely because they please or move or satisfy us*?

It is true that great music and great cathedrals give us satisfaction and pleasures. They move us.

However, we should follow Plato here, and say that great music and great cathedrals move us and please us because there is some greatness *there* that we recognize.

Not all things must be great to move us. We can get notable satisfactions from idiosyncratic things that have no greatness. Recall that I can value a chipped cup because it belonged to my grandmother. Since she mattered, she lends indirect value to the cup through my connection with her.

In the case of music and cathedrals there is no such derivation. There is no need to know who the makers or owners of the music and cathedrals are for these products to prompt satisfaction and ecstasy in many or most of us. Their value is impersonal.

Moreover, our natural intuitions are non-reductionistic here. We naturally believe that things like the Mona Lisa and the Ninth Symphony are pleasant and moving because they are things of beauty and genius. They have the sort of special *quality* that Pirsig seeks to explain in his book, *Zen and the Art of Motorcycle Maintenance*. They have a sort of value accessible to all who have an eye or ear for it. It may be impossible to define this value, but it seems real nonetheless. Pirsig himself ends up placing *quality* at a deep metaphysical level—beyond the objective-subjective division.

The fact that frogs, cats, and blind people cannot appreciate the aesthetic value present in the Mona Lisa makes no difference. They are not equipped to appreciate quality in this particular visual form. Recall that it takes recognition-capacities to notice many aspects of the real.

The same could be said of philistines. It is likely that some people with otherwise healthy senses have a curious blindness to various forms of beauty. They are as blind with respect to beauty, as otherwise healthy sadists are blind with respect to others' pain.

It takes a recognition-capacity to notice the beautiful and the great in any field. Not having it does not make the unnoticed greatness absent.

30
The value of products. Part two

Our fable needs to indulge in this new philosophical digression a little more. We have claimed that the value of our great products lies in more than feelings.

We have claimed that most of us recognize beauty and greatness in many fields.

Can we say more about this alleged recognition-capacity for the beautiful and the great?

Yes, and we can begin by noticing that all around us are forms of this recognition-capacity at work.

Virtually all of us easily recognize the difference between music and traffic noise. Virtually all of us can pick out the improved version, over the rough draft version, of a poem, a building, a painting, a room's decor.

We recognize improvement. We work on drafts with the goal of improving them. Our work almost always presupposes that there is the better and the worse, quality and shoddiness.

The better and worse applies to virtually everything—from the soundness of houses and legal cases to the elegance and beauty of music and poetry.

We could not recognize better and worse unless we already have some standard of greatness in mind that we implicitly use. Without such implicit standard things of the same kind would simply be different, neither better nor worse. We may not be able to define beauty and greatness generally. Yet we recognize it, all around us.

Let's take beauty, the most controversial form of greatness. And let's further focus on visual beauty.

None of us wants our homes to face dark and broken down alleys. We want to face fields of flowers, wide panoramas, green forests, blue seas. We all prefer elegant clothes to shabby and stained ones.

It is true that different cultures help to shape esthetic tastes in somewhat different ways. Chinese art and clothing developed along different lines than African or European art and clothing. Even among individuals in the same culture some will like Jazz and some will like Country music. Tastes do differ.

Yet in each category of art or clothing or architecture, even across cultures, there will be the better and the worse, the high and the low quality. This is an old Platonic observation.

Most of us, including persons of little taste for Chinese landscape painting, will recognize the difference in quality between a first draft of a Chinese landscape painting and an improved version.

We must not let differences in taste mislead us. Such differences are indeed accidental, individual, or culture-based. However, we must not confuse having or lacking a taste for an entire genre, with quality-recognition of items in that genre. We might not like horror movies, but we might still separate high-quality from low-quality horror movies with ease. A fanatic atheist might be turned off by all cathedrals. The same atheist might easily distinguish between the mediocre and the great Gothic ones. Something else is at work here beside the pleasure that great works can provide.

The relativity of taste proves little regarding the objectivity of quality issues. Works of quality and greatness can prompt little pleasure and satisfaction in those who have little taste for the entire category.

This would mean that even in cases of the intense pleasures prompted by great horror movies or great cathedrals it might be the greatness that explains the pleasure, not the reverse.

31
Real versus phony accomplishing
61-66, 73-76, 87-94

Let's assume that great things, accomplishments of value, are real, and that their greatness is not reducible to feeling.

We turn to the second question posed earlier, dealing not with the outcome, but with the process of accomplishing great things. Does this process of active accomplishing carry value? And if it does, does it do so because of the satisfactions we *feel* while accomplishing great things? Or is there something more?

As in the case of the greatness of products, we should reject attempts to reduce the value of our active accomplishing to mere feelings.

It is true that feelings of satisfaction accompany our efforts and successes, particularly when we succeed in the face of real challenges and perils. It is also true that these feelings themselves carry value. However, we clearly want more than these feelings and this kind of feeling-value.

The well-known experience-machine test makes this point. Here is a version of this imaginative test.

You are guaranteed a life of pleasant, satisfying, even occasionally ecstatic experiences if you only hook yourself to a life-long experience-machine. Among your experiences will be the sense of winning difficult games, climbing dangerous mountains, conquering and loving your chosen partner, and so forth. Would you do it? You could set the machine to whatever rate of felt successes and failures you like so as to maximize the intensity of the successes and of the overall experience-machine life. You could have the experience of a great and long life—even one where you experience yourself heroically helping others. It would, of course only be a dream-life. Yet it would be as vivid as real life. The experiences of dangerous mountain-climbs would be exact duplicates of real ones. Being in the machine-world would remove the uncertainties of real life. Naturally, there could be *felt* uncertainties in the machine-life, to enhance the thrills of subsequent successes. In terms of overall felt amounts of satisfactions, it would far outdo real living, even if one were to compare equally long lives.

Would you opt for the more subjectively satisfying experience-machine life over your real life?

Most of us would not opt for the experience-machine life, even knowing that our real lives carry much greater physical, psychological, and moral risks.

That is partly because we want the reality factor, an actual connection with others and with an independent world. Part of wanting the reality factor is our wanting to actually produce our accomplishments, and not merely have the sensations of producing accomplishments. Here the mere feelings of choosing, of effort, of overcoming resistance, are not enough. These feelings could be programmed features of the experience-machine-world. We want those feelings, but we also want to be the genuine agents behind the feelings.

We want to earn the feelings of satisfaction that come with accomplishing.

We will have to say more about the exact nature of this genuine agency that we so prize. In its highest form it is tied to advanced free will. In its simpler forms it is tied simply to doing, in contrast with things merely happening. The difference at basic levels is between our lifting our foot, and our food being lifted for us. It is the difference between our guiding our attention and its being guided by something else.

Doing or activeness is so basic as to be mysterious. Like beauty, we have a difficult time defining it. Yet it is both real and important. It would take a lot for us to be willing to sacrifice it. A life mainly of horror and suffering might do it, but that would in fact be a lot.

Scenarios in which we would trade away this genuine agency only indicate that there are other ultimate values. Obviously subjective happiness counts also. Nonetheless, the value of agency is more than a matter of the satisfying *feeling* of agency.

32
Agency

We are still digressing into the varied forms of fundamental value. We know, according to our fable, that the gods would seek the enhancement of value, perhaps even maximal enhancements.

We have seen that value is enhanced in many ways. It is enhanced by means of unique experiences, like the first bite of a hot pizza or the first sip of a good wine. It is also enhanced by means of great outcomes, like the painting *Mona Lisa* or Buena Vista Social Club's song *Chan Chan*. It is further enhanced through engaging in actual agency.

This latter value-source, agency, points at a related value: the value of autonomy, of self-making, made possible by advanced free will.

Being an autonomous center of agency involves more than the actual doing of an act, like climbing the mountain or taking the jump shot or biting the pizza. Yes, we want to really do these things, not merely feel that we are doing them, as the experience-machine test shows. But we want even more. We want to be able to shape the very motives from which come our important choices.

There is what can be called shallow free will, and then there is advanced free will. This latter is the form that can usher in some significant self-shaping (or autonomy).

We want to be able to act as we wish. Doing so may involve only a shallow form of free will.

Animals can have this shallow freedom when free to do as they wish. So can children. Conscious beings that cannot reflect on their own impulses and motivation can have this freedom.

It is a shallow because the desires of animals and children are set for them by nature or by external training. The agents themselves have little say in setting or reshaping their central wants. Even animals in the wild are not free in the advanced sense. Lower ranking citizens of Brave New

World also possess only this kind of freedom, since they do not get the chance to set or reshape their wants.

Animals, children, and lower ranking citizens of Brave New World do choose and act, and to some degree their choices are unpredictable. They possess the naked power of deciding one way or the other. But such choices rely on a motivational scope that is set for them by nature and circumstances.

Nonetheless, their choices are genuine and ultimate. They do involve an ultimate and controlled opting. When undecided as to which scent to follow, which toy to play with, which food to eat, they themselves resolve the ambivalence. Their choice is an ultimate doing. It is not a happening like a random coin-flip occurring in their mind. A coin-flip is not in the agent's control. This opting-action is, instead, the agent's doing.

What is this agent-controlled opting? Ultimately this is hard to say. It might be linked to quantum statistical randomness, but it cannot be simply a matter of this randomness.

The agent-control involved in choosing option A instead of option B seems to be its own primitive and indefinable reality. Yet we all recognize it. It may even be attached to all levels of consciousness.

We have seen that the world needs this sort of power. It needs it so that some choices are both done and are done unpredictably. The world needs agents that yield surprises.

By itself this power of agent-control produces a level of unpredictable free will, even if shallow.

Yet there is a more advanced level of freedom, where the agent does not simply act within the scope of desires and impulses set by nature or others. At more advanced levels freedom permits the agent to set its inner motivational scope to at least some degree.

33
Agency and advanced free will

We are now exploring the kind of freedom that may enable some degree of self-shaping. It is worth noting that not even the gods can engage in a total self-shaping. A being must already exist, and have some urges, for it to further shape itself. But some partial self-shaping seems possible. This is what we are after.

We have seen that a primitive opting power produces some degree of unpredictable and controlled origination on our part and on the part of animals.

But we want more. We want to set our own wants. We don't want to act merely within bounds of impulses, wants, needs, values, or preferences, which have been set for us by nature or by culture. We want a hand in our own programming.

It is true that each of us has no choice regarding our initial sets of inclinations, longings, and values. Nature, genes, and culture set these. Yet, at some point, if we can engage in a certain type of reflection, and do so in the right way, we might have a shot at reshaping ourselves on our own.

The crucial factors for this advanced free will and self-reshaping are reflection and sufficient judging resources.

As humans we generally acquire the capacity to reflect on our own inner life, including our motives and impulses. Attaining an advanced level of free will involves being able to direct this reflection ourselves. This we can do so long we are not manipulated by hypnotists or evil demons.

The part about having sufficient judging resources is more complex. It requires individual access to a number of alternative values and goals.

We must, in reflecting, have some leeway as to which values and goals to make central to our lives.

Merely reflecting on our initial set of wants and impulses and values has no point, unless we have some goal or standard in mind. Looking at our own motives merely to look at them, would not give us any control of motives. We also need to be able to assess initial motives. At minimum, we must be able to recognize the inconsistencies and the insanity of some of our motives. Only so would we be prompted to act upon them, and thus acquire some control of our motives.

For example, if an agent has a powerful desire for a life mainly of alcohol or gambling, that agent must recognize that this is not a healthy desire. Recognition of crazy or healthy motives requires our possessing standards of craziness or health.

Now comes the hard part. What about the standards or goals themselves? We need to have some choice about these, or else we would control our motives only by means of factors over which we have no control.

Perhaps if we have access to a variety of such standards and life-goals, if they compete for our limited time, and if they are of similar strength, then their clashes would cause us to pause and reflect about them. Which of them do we want to be our main life-guide? This might give us some ultimate control.

Here is a case where such ultimate control is mostly absent:

Imagine that one of us, Amir, at some point in his youth begins to feel natural sexual urges. Imagine that Amir reflects on these desires guided by the value-judgment that all sexual impulses are immoral. Amir acquired this value-judgment in a strict and narrow culture (this has happened many times). Amir was pressured to judge this way by parents, peers, and teachers, on pain of severe social rejection. He was told not to trust his natural valuing of sexual pleasure. Amir then reflects on his surging sexual impulses, and finds them evil. In such a case, Amir's own reflection will condemn his sexual desires.

Amir reflects and chooses here, but not on the basis of a value standard over which he had much control. Thus, his deliberate repression of sexual impulses cannot be said to be deeply free.

34
Reflection and multiple value standards

We are still investigating the kind of reflection that is friendly to advanced freedom, or to autonomy.

Not all reflection regarding our own motives contributes to our autonomy.

At a minimum a person like Amir must be aware of a number of possible options as value-standards or life-goals. Amir must then reflect on these options.

Autonomy requires some reflection directed at the standards themselves. We must have some leeway in this reflection. We must have access to a wide enough array of goals and standards (that play a role in this reflection).

It is our good fortune that our human natural inclinations—before cultural interferences—appear to be multiple and democratic. We are naturally inclined towards many different life-pursuits. These inclinations do not generally dictate any particular life-goal, and they presuppose recognition of multiple values.

This makes possible the necessary leeway for reflective self-shaping.

We naturally long for beauty, or sensory pleasures, or curiosity and exploration, or love and friendship, or power and self-assertion, or play and music and humor, or social justice. There may be other natural longings. Which of these should we make our central life pursuit(s)? The multiplicity of these inclinations alone—even when affected by individual variations—is likely to spur periodic conflicts and reflection, since a person cannot develop all of these pursuits in a single lifetime.

Reflection combined with our basic opting power, over time, will help determine whether one will follow mainly the longing for a life of play, or the longing for a life of love and devotion, or the longing for a life of study. Our repeated introspection might also lead us to a life that combines these goals.

The reflecting process must allow us some leeway, at least at key junctures. Do I follow my impulse to please and to listen to my parents, in choosing engineering as my main field? Or do I follow my impulse for independence and art, so that I can pursue a career in painting?

Broad upbringings and broad educations generally help in this reflective self-formation, by encouraging the exploration of different possibilities. However, an open education is not always available. In narrow and repressive families or societies, significant autonomy will be much more difficult to achieve.

It will be difficult, but not impossible, so long as our natural inclinations, and the inner standards they imply, are not completely stifled.

In the case of Amir, at least with respect to sexual pleasure, his own natural reflective resources are stifled. Even though he assesses his sexual motives, his assessment process is itself unfree.

The process is unfree because he is not encouraged to reflect on, and determine, his own central values (at least in this one area). Instead, Amir is systematically pressured—almost forced—to abandon the natural recognition of pleasure as a good.

35
Autonomy and the role of culture

Can we say more regarding the role of society with respect to our partial self-shaping?

Societies have not always been friendly toward autonomy. Societies do not always encourage its members to examine alternative basic values and ways of life. Societies can be, and have been, narrow and rigid. Narrow societies will not encourage examining multiple value standards.

Yet it appears that even in narrow and rigid societies, individuals have a chance at advanced free will and at some degree of self-shaping. Some individuals always escape cultural straitjackets, and become free thinkers. Even narrow dark ages eventually unveil resources that lead to renaissances. Some independent thought and judgment somehow survive such periods.

These facts suggest that individuals must have inner and natural resources that can broaden narrow cultural value-teachings.

We must have a common human capacity to recognize crazy beliefs and practices, even when all around us insist that these beliefs and practices are natural and blessed by the gods.

This natural recognition and capacity for sanity—a natural and intuitive understanding of value, as Plato maintained—can pave the way for some advanced freedom even in culturally stifling circumstances.

We must remind ourselves that our natural impulses are not confined to desire for food, sleep, and warmth! We are naturally very complex.

We are equipped with natural, broad, and healthy inclinations for things of value. We have as natural a leaning towards things of value, as we do towards language acquisition.

As mentioned before, we naturally seek the following: beauty, varieties of sensory pleasures, knowledge and exploration, love and friendship of many forms, survival and self-assertion and power, empathy and love and fairness, play and music and humor.

Being inclined in these directions implies that we have an eye for the corresponding objects. We must have some idea of what we are seeking when seeking beauty and love, or else we would not recognize the right objects when they cross our path. This too is an old Platonic point.

In fact, we do have a natural eye for symmetry and beauty, a feel for games and adventure, a sense for the love or the happiness of others. These natural recognitions can supply us with innate standards of judgment.

The evidence of children is undeniable here. When children are not too strictly stifled, their natural tastes for play, beauty, and knowledge develops naturally. This natural development mirrors that of language-acquisition, which is also enabled by a natural proclivity for it.

A child's natural recognition of multiple values, when not stifled, can later play a role in guiding reflection regarding which desires to promote and follow.

These natural inclinations and recognition capacities give us a shot at both autonomy and sanity.

A woman in traditional societies is often pressured into a single role—to be a devoted daughter, wife, and daughter in law. If our picture is correct, even such a woman has a shot at examining her natural impulses toward play, art, independence, knowledge, without automatically dismissing these. Social pressures to have her dismiss these impulses will find natural resistance. Her natural recognition for the value of knowledge, independence, power, play, art, will have to be overcome.

In a very strict culture she is likely to submit to local values. Still, her natural value-resources may generate enough of a reflective struggle to give her a chance to partly shape herself.

36
Autonomy and the sacred individual

If the thrust of the preceding account of partial autonomy is correct, it helps explain why most humans are uniquely special. Unlike dogs and dolphins, most humans have reflective powers that can help the shaping of their own characters, their main life-goals, and thus the impulses behind their choices.

As a consequence of this special reflective power, humans can be centers not only of doings but of unpredictable doings. They can also be centers of ultimately self-directed doings.

We remain, of course, centers of inner experiences. Thus, we carry value on different accounts.

We feel. We do. We (can) do autonomously.

The presence of unpredictable agents, even if possessing only shallow freedom, fits within the picture of a world of interest to the gods because it ushers in the element of adventure and self-propelled surprise. Autonomous agency fits into a world in which the central characters—each of us, for example—can help to shape themselves and their main life-directions. The element of Platonic values-intuition helps to make this unpredictable self-shaping both non-arbitrary and non-crazy.

The gods would indeed want to feel unique sensations and complex emotions through us. However, they would also want new and genuinely produced twists in our stories. The gods would not be satisfied with some absolute randomness added to story-twists and phony agency in experience-machine-worlds. This mere randomness would only produce unpredictable happenings—though felt as doings. It would not produce unpredictable *genuine* doings. It certainly would not produce genuinely autonomous doings.

These latter doings carry the special mark of partial self-creation. Our lives are living pictures that we, while inside the initial drafts of the pictures, help to form by using some of our reflective agency in unpredictable but non-arbitrary ways.

There will be natural questions here. Isn't our whole world one that is currently being imagined by some god, as our fable has been supposing? If so, how different is our world from a massive experience-machine world? How can we know if we are real active characters, and not mere machine-world characters who feel as though they are real and active?

We must answer, again, that not being able to tell the difference between our being real and our being machine-world characters is not a problem. At the feeling-level there would be no difference—a dream-pain within a dream hurts as much as a real pain in real life. The possibility that the whole world is ultimately being imagined, and is made up of divine mental imaginative stuff—even when the mental stuff looks and feels like snow and rock—does not matter. What matters is that such an imaginative god would be after many types of value.

We have seen that live feeling-value is one type of value. But genuine agency-value is another. A god aiming at values would want to imagine, or become, characters with *real* powers, including independent powers of genuine agency. Such characters are much more interesting!

Even if ultimately all is made up of imaginative mental stuff, it is a safe bet that we have real agency powers. Some of us are bound to have some degree of genuine autonomy-powers.

Thus, it is almost certain that we are genuine and independent individuals, and that many of us are part-authors of our own programming and story. As such we are each special. We might even count as sacred.

37
Sacred individuals

So, if both our fable and our experience can be trusted, we are likely to be not only centers of consciousness and feeling, but also individuals with real autonomous agency powers.

We feel. We do. We do with some freedom. We (can) do autonomously.

The first three capacities we share with many non-human animals. The last one may be a uniquely human capacity.

It may not be the only uniquely human capacity. We also have astonishing powers of imagination. We can imagine what is not here, and what does not exist. We can imagine different versions of ourselves, and different versions of our social world. This helps us to add new dimensions both to ourselves and to our world.

Reflection and imagination help us to change our looks, our skills, and even our desires. We deliberately lose weight, turn vegan, take up the violin.

Reflection and imagination help us to change our world and enrich it in countless ways. We help extend daylight with electricity. We organize complex networks of exchanges that permit us to trade a tiny fraction of our labor for some pounds of avocados produced worlds away. In fiction, particularly in fantasy and science fiction—not to mention virtual machine-worlds—we even imagine worlds that bend the framework boundaries of our common world.

It is not clear whether humans are the only beings with imaginative powers. Many other animals seem to plan, store, travel, build. These activities may involve imagining what is not present, and then taking steps to make the imagined state real. To say that beavers built damns, birds build nests, and spiders weave webs by programmed instinct gives these animals little credit. It treats them as robots devoid of inner lives. What we call instinct may be consistent with some intelligence and some imagination.

Nonetheless, it is safe to say that the scale of our human imagination, helped by our complex language-capacity, makes our advantage over non-humans an immense one. Our imagination leads to almost infinite levels of abstraction from our present bodily and sensory experience. It can identify prime numbers and prove that there must be an infinite number of them. Our imagination has countless types of application—it invents social utopias, new flying machines, and new ways of using wind power.

Our imagination, as we saw, goes so far as to turn on itself, in helping to reshape the inner character of the imaginative agent.

Are the combined powers of imagination and autonomous reflective agency what make us unique, special, and perhaps even sacred? ...Or spiritual? ...Or divine?

The latter terms are obscure. However, if they mean something like god-like, then they might be appropriate.

We are likely to be imitations, images, smaller-scale versions, of gods.

Just as a god is a conscious being that freely imagines and acts in accord with value-enhancing goals, so we too can freely imagine and act in accord (in part) with value-enhancing goals.

In imagining different possible futures for ourselves, in envisaging better worlds, in inventing new songs, etc., we engage in imaginative and creative activities that partake of the divine.

Our being made in god's image may have a profound element of truth. However, we must not forget that feeling is just as divine. Part of the reason for divine and human imaginings is to expand the range of felt experiences.

38
Sacred individuals. Part two

We have thus far identified at least three basic sources of value. Two have to do with our qualities—having a qualitative inner life, and being agents and autonomous originators. One has to do with the quality of our outcomes and products.

We saw that a qualitative inner life has a self-mattering status. As such it carries value.

How does agency or autonomous agency, even when combined with extensive imagination, carry value? Does it do so by imitating a divine activity—hence the use of terms like "sacred"? Perhaps, but why does that divine activity, in turn, carry intrinsic worth.

Where is the self-mattering part when it comes to this strange agency?

The answer cannot be that agency is a special tool because it yields new things, new music, new beauty, or even new universes with independent mini-agents. A special tool is still only a tool, and carries no intrinsic worth.

We could say that autonomous agency must have independent value, since none of us would give it up in favor of a richer inner life of a machine-world (which could include the phony impression of agency). However, this answer only shows that it is something great. But what makes it so great?

Is it that free and autonomous agency makes possible moral responsibility? Is it that in choosing among genuinely open and imagined possibilities, and in being partial self-shapers, no other force in the universe directs and controls some of the outcomes in our lives? Is it that it makes us ongoing part-authors of ourselves?

These reasons seem merely to be reformulations of what it is to be autonomous agents. To say that being autonomous is great because of the feature of autonomy is not to explain anything. Nor does it help to add that in being partly autonomous agents we are beings that escape any final definition, in that we can always further redefine ourselves. Nor does it help to say that we are unique individuals that yield ongoing surprises in a world worthy of divine participation. Surprise could be attained through shallow free will alone.

We might have to conclude that autonomy is simply another unique and non-reducible value.

Autonomy might be a value so basic that it cannot be explained in terms of some other yet more basic value. It might be another primitive value, like that of consciousness and feeling. This is our best suggestion.

We value consciousness. We value pleasure. We value agency, and advanced free will. We value beauty and quality. We clearly want other things for the sake of each of these. Yet these values we want (at least partly) for their own sakes. These values simply cannot be further explained.

We simply must conclude that these values are ultimate or primitive values.

Ultimate or not, the fact remains that those of us with the capacity for autonomous agency have an additional source of worth. We may have a specialness that brings us closer to the full specialness of gods.

Presumably, a simple divine command would follow from this shared status: respect yourselves and each other. At a minimum, such a command would ask that we not violate each other. The same command might require that we go further and that we help each other flourish.

These possible commands we'll have to spell out.

39
Human sacredness and divine sacredness

So, we have seen that we are real individuals who have a subjective life, and who also can have autonomous agency powers. We may indeed have a specialness that is akin to the specialness of gods.

Can we use this resemblance to say more about the gods?

Let's dare again to do so.

We have seen that the gods must have inner lives and intentions. They must aim at value. Among the values at which they must aim is the value of autonomous agency.

It would be surprising if the value of autonomous agency resided only in imagined agents present in imagined worlds. If this value is so special, the gods themselves would possess it.

It is true that some intrinsic values, like those linked with visual beauty or music, are tied to specific worlds and specific senses. A god cannot be said to look good, even if it might seek forms of visual beauty that in turn require specific senses.

But agency, like consciousness or feeling, relates to the inner character of a god, not to the contents, outcomes, products, of its imaginings and worlds.

As we saw before, a god whose only state is permanent bliss is too much like an experience-machine god. Even a perfect version of an experience-machine passive god falls short of a genuine god. An experience-machine god would subjectively feel the most perfect feelings, and the most perfect permanent high. However, such a god would lack the agency-value that we prize for ourselves and that is linked with nobility.

Could gods possess simple agency powers, the powers to opt this way or that, and not possess the self-shaping power of autonomous agency? Could we be more worthy, in this respect, than the gods?

This cannot be. We must presume that genuine gods are also carriers of the value of autonomous agency. In fact, we must presume that they carry such value to a much higher degree than we do.

What would this imply?

It would imply that gods have advanced powers of imagination and of self-reflection. These powers, we noticed, must have played a role in the imaginative formation of worlds.

More interestingly, self-shaping must imply that a god is not "initially" fully shaped—whether by nature or by others.

In order to have the power of autonomous self-shaping a god would have to "start off" being incomplete, and perfectible. It would have to have unfinished inclinations in multiple value-directions. It, too, would have to escape being subject to some narrow inner-value dictatorship. Its self-perfecting process would have to be governed by a naked free will power and by some array of different and democratic inclinations and values.

It too would need some reflective and motivational latitude regarding which overall goals to promote.

Perhaps the scope of its initial values, in the case of a god, is immense. Perhaps some such values are beyond our range of comprehension.

Nonetheless, some unfinished constitution must be part of the inner divine nature for gods to be at least as (partly) incomprehensible and noble as we are.

40
Unfinished gods

We saw that an unfinished constitution must be part of the inner divine nature, for gods to be at least as noble as we are.

This should not surprise us.

We saw before that a live god is a dynamic god; and that a dynamic god cannot be a perfectly finished god. Put differently, divine perfection must involve aliveness. And the highest form of aliveness must in turn involve not only the unveiling of previously non-existing worlds, but also the form-ing of a previously unformed self-character.

A noble god is one that gets credit for turning itself into something great—or else its greatness would be just a matter of luck.

Many have claimed that a god must be good essentially. That is, the goodness of a god must be a natural part of its make-up. If it were so, however, this goodness would not have been earned. But, then, the goodness freely earned by our best humans would be more meritorious than that of this essentially good god. This is because the goodness of our best humans is one that is freely acquired, and need not have been. It is a virtue that has withstood challenges. An essentially good god would just be lucky to be good.

This cannot be. Our best humans cannot be more meritorious than a genuine god. A divine goodness must, therefore, also be freely acquired. This means that a divine goodness must originate from a field of multiple inclinations, some of which might be morally neutral. Might some even be destructive?

We could speculate that the "original" nature of a god inclines toward multiple objectives like power, beauty, and sheer creativity, independently of the forms these impulses could take. Perhaps such a god could have opted for imagined worlds of beautiful robotic characters, simply to exhibit its immense and neutral power. It could have freely invented worlds of mere aesthetic beauty independently of any moral dimension (which requires inner lives and agency).

That our world, instead, includes beings like us, beings with inner lives and independent agency powers, beings worthy of respect, might be a credit to a god's resisting or mitigating these other alternate impulses.

Or it could be that the inclusion of beings like us is not a matter of mere self-enrichment but of a most noble from of divine self-enrichment, as we have been claiming.

Our inclusion in imagined worlds could be both self-enriching and credit-worthy for gods. This would assume that a god is capable of pursuing the lesser value instead of the greater value, and in some sense freely opts for the greater. We are more risky because more independent. We are also more satisfying for a god to be.

Sure, these are intellectually difficult and speculative waters.

In any case, we saw that divine world-imaginings are likely to be vehicles for value-enhancement. Simultaneously, these world-imaginings may be expressions of autonomous agency-value on the part of a god. They may be vehicles through which a divine being shapes or re-shapes itself, in accord with some combination of its multiple, "natural," and undeveloped value-inclinations.

How this last part would happen, and the prerequisites for a divine reshaping, must remain somewhat obscure. *That* this divine self-shaping happens, so as to make a god into a credit-worthy agent, might have to be a reality.

This need for divine self-shaping aligns well with the presence of our world! A work of art can contribute in reshaping the artist's character. A god's imagining of itself in a world like ours may contribute to a god's reshaping of itself.

41
Human sacredness and animal sacredness

Let's return to two of the basic sources of inner value we have so far investigated—having a qualitative inner life, and being (autonomous) agents.

We are likely to share both of these features with the gods. In being thus god-like we are similarly sacred. What does this say of our non-human cousins around us? What if animals have reduced versions of these inner qualities? Are they non-sacred?

Not so fast.

Let's notice some obvious facts.

Each of the two basic values we have just mentioned—having a qualitative inner life, and being an autonomous agent—can be more or less complex. Each can be possessed to a smaller or to a greater degree.

Non-human animals have some inner life. The inner lives of animals perhaps contain less variety than our inner life has. Animals don't feel anxiety about losses of jobs or about the loss of youth. Yet their inner lives might also be more focused and intense. The olfactory sensations of dogs must make ours seem very dull. They may even possess senses unique to their species. Birds may sense magnetic fields, perhaps in the way we sense sound waves.

Non-human animals certainly possess agency powers, but perhaps not reflective autonomy powers (they cannot reflect on and re-shape their own impulses and characters themselves). They are likely to have limited imaginations, and are thus more confined to their present moments, circumstances, and inclinations. What they dream about, we may not know, but presumably even in dreams their range of experiences is narrower than ours is.

History indicates that we vastly underestimate the range of animal powers. The more closely we study them, particularly by forming long-term close bonds with them, the more they surprise us. Their inner powers may be more complex that we think. For instance, according to the research of biologist Rupert Sheldrake, many ordinary dogs have tele-pathic powers. Some have been filmed as sensing the precise moment their human friend decides to come home, even if the decision is made at irregular times.

For current purposes, however, let's keep our assumptions modest. Let us suppose that the inner lives and the agency-powers of non-human animals are generally much simpler and more limited than ours.

Even so, we must notice a basic continuum in powers among ani-mals, and between humans and animals.

Among non-human animals the level of complexity of inner expe-rience and agency powers is likely to vary substantially. The inner life and the agency powers of dolphins will have little resemblance to the inner life and agency powers of frogs or sparrows, not to mention wasps and ants.

We must also note that a similar range of inner complexity levels occurs among humans. We differ widely in talent and handicap levels. Some humans, the seriously mentally disabled, have very limited inner lives. Some, though a small minority, have no power of self-reflection and of autonomous agency at all.

Thus, even if we grant that non-humans generally have much simp-ler inner lives, we cannot fail to note that the totality of earthly lives, across species, forms a continuum of inner complexity and powers. The sharp traditional distinction between humans and non-humans—we are special, they are not—that we have traditionally accepted is based on a considerable distortion.

We also cannot fail to note that having a qualitative inner life, even a simpler one, counts independently of other values. In light of these complications, who counts as sacred?

It is not so easy to say.

42
Human sacredness and animal sacredness. Part two

We have seen that earthly beings form a continuum in terms of complexity of both inner lives and agency powers. This continuum cuts across species. The traditional sharp division between humans and non-humans is a bias-induced distortion. It is not supported by an inspection of how capacities are distributed.

This distortion has led most human traditions to treat all animals as tools or resources for us. Outside of the Buddhist and Jain traditions, most of us have not considered non-humans as sacred.

There are parallels between how non-humans have been seen and how people of other races have been seen by even the brightest minds in our own western traditions. Often we have used terms like animal, beast, and savage, as devices to devalue humans who are different from our in-group.

What has been said of "savages" and of racially different humans by otherwise sensitive and perceptive thinkers—from Kant, to Hegel, to Jefferson—is a sad commentary on how foolish even the best of us can be.

It should have been obvious all along that humans of different skin color and of different cultural traditions have inner lives and advanced agency-powers much like those of one's own group.

It should have been equally obvious that many, perhaps all, non-human animals have some inner life and some agency powers. There are obvious continuities here. Some non-humans are more able in the areas of inner life and agency powers than are humans with serious mental impairments.

Important thinkers, like Emmanuel Kant, have attributed sacredness only to those beings capable of significant autonomous agency, and have tried to use this trait to separate all humans from all non-humans.

However, this ignores the fact that a minority of humans lacks the capacity for autonomous agency. It ignores the even more basic fact that inner life counts even when unaccompanied by reflective agency-powers.

One need only think of our brain-damaged child, and of our favorite cat or dog—or any cat or dog, if we remove our morally puzzling nepotism. One need only imagine future robots suddenly infused with a real consciousness and a capacity for pleasure and pain.

To feel is to count. Those who feel must matter!

Our pro-human perspective often forgets that a unique inner life—whether of humans or aliens, of bats or alligators—by itself adds value to the universe.

Does this mean that beings of more limited inner lives and more limited agency count to the same degree as beings of more complex inner lives and agency? ... Or, if more limited inner lives were to count less, how much less? Does value come in degrees? Does it come in lower and higher forms?

Is there an absolute threshold above which beings are sacred, and below which beings are not sacred? Are we willing to consider those humans who will fall below the threshold as not sacred? Does sacredness come in degrees?

The notions behind these questions—degrees of value and cut-off lines for sacredness—are puzzling.

For now, we need only insist on recognizing the value-status of the less able humans and of sentient animals. We must at least accept that value-status extends beyond the category of beings with advanced free will.

It is a considerable act of human vanity to think that the gods would use only humans as vehicles of value-enrichment. With our imaginative powers we should have transcended this myopic view long ago.

43
Sacredness and duties of moral agents

We have seen that most of us who have advanced free will and imagination carry more responsibility. Among such responsibility is that of treating at least some others with respect. Respect entails non-harming—at least non-harming innocent others. Respect might also entail helping the less fortunate.

We need to say more regarding which others fall within the range of our duties.

We need to say more regarding whether these others exert equal pull on our duties.

We have not established what institutional or social forms these duties should take.

Complex ethics debates surround each of these issues. We can only touch on some of these debates.

We start by noting that moral duties are present only for those capable of real alternate choices. Dogs have little or no moral duties, though they can be trained to do what is right. When lions kill they do so innocently. Children and mentally less able humans at most have partial moral duties. At the other end of the continuum, those capable of mature self-control, of advanced free will, carry full moral obligations. We'll call these latter full moral agents.

Who must full moral agents respect? Clearly anyone (or anything) of intrinsic worth deserves some respect. So, we must respect not only other full moral agents, but also the less able humans and those non-humans capable of inner lives. Let's recall that inner lives carry a self-mattering quality.

Must we respect all others, of intrinsic worth, equally? This depends on whether value and sacredness come in degrees or in an all-or-nothing form. As reluctant as we might be about assigning degrees of worth to other beings out there, we might have to do so.

In practice we cannot help but value birds more than worms, fish more than bacteria, trees more than grass, elephants more than rats, humans more than chickens or trees or grass. The simple acts of feeding, clothing, and housing ourselves involves making choices as to which of these are more expendable.

The degree of complexity and range of a being's inner life is probably the rough measure we must use in making these degree judgments. Those with a more complex inner life seem to carry more worth. This measure—inner complexity—should not always favor humans in conflict cases. Those humans of unusually serious mental disabilities could have a less complex inner life than average chimps, cats, or pigs. Thus, this measure has the virtue of impartiality.

Even so, harm to beings with inner lives should be avoided and their well-being should be sought. When hard choices must be made, we must aim to minimize the harm. In conflict cases, humans or others of higher worth must be favored only if their vital interests are at stake, and not their trifling ones. The life of a rat (perhaps even of a tree) cannot be sacrificed for the passing pleasure of a chimp or of a human.

A major implication of this harm-minimizing approach—one that separates serious and trifling benefits—is that most of us humans must stop using most if not all animals for food, even if we are more worthy creatures. If we have other food options of satisfactory nutritional value, then the use of animal beings as mere food resources is an unnecessary moral abuse. Most of us do have these cruelty-free food options.

This is a serious implication in view of our continued practices. We systematically bring into the world hundreds of millions of misery-filled conscious beings, only so as to kill them at our convenience. This massive cruelty is mostly for the sake of some extra food pleasure or for the sake of maintaining dubious traditions. We could not condone this treatment, on these grounds, of our favorite dog or cat. Yet the inner lives of pigs or cows may differ little from that of our dog or cat.

Most of us do not mean to engage in unprovoked cruelties. Yet, too many of us proceed with startling indifference toward this dark underbelly of our system—the daily abuses and slaughters of millions of factory-farmed living beings. This indifference is a severe indictment of the ethical component of those religions that provide cover for these needless cruelties.

44

Sacredness and institutional duties of moral agents

Since those of us who are full moral agents are surrounded by beings of intrinsic worth, we have to honor them individually. We must also honor them through the kind of social world we construct. This obligation parallels that of gods who must construct a world that is fair to beings that, once present, carry independent value—as we will see.

Since our social world is a matter of our collective choices, what kind of social world should we construct?

This issue has been debated for thousands of years, at least as far back as Plato's *Republic*. It is basically the issue of what a just society looks like. It has at least two major components: a political one regarding who should govern, and an economic one regarding who should own what.

The political side of the issue has been more or less resolved. We have gradually come to learn that some form of popular self-government, or democracy, is the form that is most respectful of humans.

The economic side of the issue is still disputed. The economic egalitarians and the free-market non-egalitarians have been battling it out—intellectually and at times in battlefields—for a long time.

A compromise between the two is not only possible, but is morally rather self-evident.

We can see this by means of a simple, yet powerful, test that we can each conduct. The test was introduced by the recent American philosopher John Rawls. The following is a simplified variant of this test.

Imagine we are to be reborn on earth. Before we die we are each asked to choose the economic system for our next life. The important catch is that we don't know who each of us will be. That is, we don't know if we'll be male or female, short or tall, good looking or ugly, intellectually talented or stupid, naturally energetic or lazy. Thus, we would not choose a system that will mainly benefit, say, males—since half of us will be female! Not knowing our next life's gender, we would each choose a gender-neutral system.

The general lesson is that this method of picking the conditions for our next life is impartial. This method forces us to serve our interests by serving the interests of everyone, since in this next life we could be anyone of these future constituents.

We must, then, honor and be fair to everyone—by choosing what is best for our future self. Which *economic* arrangements would we choose for our next life under such impartial conditions of choice (called by Rawls "the veil of ignorance")?

To maximize our opportunities and minimize our risks, whomever we turn out to be, we would not pick a society that is excessively partial toward initial wealth or initial poverty. This is because we don't know whether we'll begin our next life in a wealthy family setting, or in a poor family setting. We don't want initial wealth-inheritance to mean a lot—because we might not inherit any such wealth! Nor do we want initial poverty to mean a lot, in terms of denied opportunities—because we might be born in a poor family.

To reduce the impact of initial wealth or poverty we would choose neither pure capitalism nor pure communism. Under pure capitalism a child would not have any guarantees regarding basic needs and opportunities. Under pure communism—one that assigns equal or common possessions to everyone—a person who contributes greatly to the community would not receive greater rewards than a non-contributor. We could be the ones making the great contributions. We would want a system that rewards special contributions (such as new inventions like the microscope or the pill or the internet) with special wealth, so as to keep encouraging such contributions.

We want a system that generates a lot of wealth, which can then be used to fund public schools…, which can in turn enable somewhat equal opportunities for each new generation. We can add, for our test, that not only we don't know *who* we will be, but we also don't know *when* we'll be reborn. Thus, we want a system rich enough to sustain both equal opportunities and basic needs guarantees across generations.

45
Sacredness and the just society

We are playing with the idea of a social system that respects everyone. Fairness must be at the core of this system. This is a matter of respecting others through our institutions.

We have seen that a self serving, yet impartial, way of selecting a system suggests that we reject economic egalitarianism, or communism. We must encourage wealth creation. Thus, we must enable those who contribute more to have a greater portion of wealth than those who contribute less. Perhaps there is some other way of encouraging wealth creation. The historical evidence seems to indicate otherwise, at least regarding large-scale communities.

The goal, in any case, is not absolute economic equality. It is fairness and respect for everyone.

A measure of fairness and respect for everyone is the manner in which a system is able to provide for the least well off, and do so for many generations (since we could have our rebirth in any future generation). It looks like providing the most for the least well off can occur only in a system that repeatedly and reliably generates plenty of wealth.

Of course, we have also seen that a pure market-system, pure capitalism, will create huge initial imbalances in children's opportunities. The poorest and least able will be guaranteed neither basic needs nor basic educational guarantees. Not knowing who we'll be in our next life—according to our test—none of us would risk choosing this all-or-nothing system.

So, for the sake of a high economic floor we need to attach large strings to private wealth acquisition. This wealth must also help to maintain a system of equal opportunity for each following generation. The wealthy future you—potentially—must be willing to donate some wealth to the community for the sake of guaranteed access to basic education, basic medical care, and basic transportation. This might mean funding for public schools and public hospitals and public roads. Alternatively, it might mean funding for subsidies so that the poor and less able can afford private schools, private hospitals, and private roads. The funding method can in turn be achieved through a graduated taxation system, or through some other way.

In addition, some limitation on inheritance would have to be instituted, to reduce the opportunity gaps among the children of each successive generation.

Unequal outcomes can be fair if attained in the right way. Unequal private wealth outcomes can be fair if attained through the right kind of honest competition. Such competition requires somewhat equal starting points. For instance, poorer but talented children should not be at a significant disadvantage compared to richer and talented children. Fair competition requires a high degree of equal opportunities for all. In realistic terms, we must at least reduce the initial inequalities as much as is reasonably possible.

We have been assuming, in our imaginative test, that we'll be born in a world like ours, one that includes initial natural inequalities. Some will still be born talented, and some a lot less so. We don't want to add another source of starting-point inequality by having richer children have much greater opportunities than poorer children. The right system must aim at equal cultural starting points. Equal educational preparation and opportunities are central to such equal cultural starting points. Equal starting points are, in turn, an important step on the way to full fairness.

Let's also recall that unequal wealth outcomes might be necessary to keep creating wealth to sustain the funding of a high floor of basic needs for everyone. Such unequal outcomes are also needed to fund the very system of equal successive opportunities for everyone. The historical record indicates that large-scale societies that have tried to eliminate wealth inequalities have not created higher economic floors, compared to other more unequal societies. If so, we must embrace some inequalities of wealth-outcomes.

All in all, it appears that the economic system we would all select for our next life, not knowing who we would be, is some version of the mixed system—a mixture of capitalism and socialism. This makes the mixed economic system the fairest one.

46
Sacredness and the just society. Part two

We have argued, based on an imaginative test, that the mixed economic system is the fairest one. If the mixed economic system is fair, and is the one we would all impartially select for our next life, there should be even today some real-world confirmation.

In fact, as already stated, we have considerable real-world confirmation for this imaginative result.

We have had societies where people have more or less freely chosen system-features through their votes. When they have done so over a long period of time, so that their collective choices are tested by real-world implications, all democratic societies have opted for some version of the mixed economic system.

The US, France, Sweden, Japan, and in fact all of the successful and democratic countries where people have expressed their choices over a long period of time, have opted for some version of this system.

The fairness of the mixed economic system is somewhat self-evident, after all! And people are not stupid—at least they cannot be fooled forever.

The Soviet dictatorship only fooled and oppressed people for some time. Eventually people began to demand political and economic freedoms. The unregulated free-marketism of late 1800's America could only fool people for some time. Then people began to demand minimal public schools for all children, minimally safe and humane working conditions, and minimal old age pensions. Even in more free-market leaning countries like the US of today, the idea of public schools for all is widely accepted. Institutions such as Medicare, Medicaid, and Social Security are not fundamentally disputed. The debates over universal basic health care possibilities are a small anomaly among advanced democratic countries.

There are differences from one advanced democratic country to the next, as to the exact mix of market factors and public sectors. However, these are differences over details, not principle. Few, if any, dispute the need for some mix of private and public sectors. Even those humane libertarian voices who would prefer, say, an all-private system of education, would want public subsidies to enable poor children to afford access to basic private schooling.

The precisely correct balance between the role of public and of private sectors may not be easy to determine. Yet here, too, current results point in certain definite directions.

We have something called the UN Human Development Index. It ranks countries in terms of three combined factors: wealth per capita, average life expectancy, and average educational achievement. These are plausible, if very rough, standards for measuring social success. According to these factors the top countries year after year tend to be countries like Norway, Switzerland, Canada, Australia, and Sweden.

These are all democratic countries. And, more interestingly, these countries have generous welfare-state policies that help to yield high floors for the worst off. These countries also have sufficiently high wealth-generation to be able to back up these generous policies.

Among actual countries these come closest to the model-system that we would each pick for our next life. They are the most Rawlsian countries.

It seems, then, that the combination of a mixed economic system combined and a democratic political system is the way to go, if we seek to respect ourselves and others through our chosen social institutions.

47
Sacredness and the just society. Part three

We have seen that those of us who are full moral agents must honor the beings around us that have intrinsic worth. We must honor them individually but also institutionally—through the kind of social world we construct.

We have also seen that adopting some form of the mixed economic system is the way to respect everyone when it comes to issues of wealth and poverty.

We have, finally, noted that some form of democracy will treat everyone with respect, by giving everyone a voice in governing. In fact, it is through sustained periods of democracy that people historically end up selecting mixed economic policies. Oligarchies and monarchies have not generally been friendly to those at the socio-economic bottom.

None of us would opt for non-democratic governments in a future society, if we did not know who we will be in that society. Political democracy passes Rawls' selection test.

Recall, however, that a mixed economic system allows for some inequality of wealth. Even a fair mixed system could allow for a significantly unequal distribution of wealth—so long as this distribution also benefits the worst off the most, and does not deny equal opportunities to young people.

Unfortunately, unequal wealth creates a chronic danger for democracy. Wealthy voices find ways of counting more than the voices of the poorer in shaping governing policies. 'One person, one vote' often ends up becoming 'more wealth, more votes.' Thus, barriers need to be in place separating private wealth from government influence. These barriers have proven to be extremely difficult to establish.

One solution is some form of direct democracy (a referenda system). A second solution is an indirect democracy with public financing of campaigns; or an indirect democracy featuring permanent wealth-bans on high government officers (as Plato long ago suggested).

Sustained respect for everyone's voice calls for one of these solutions, or for a combination of these. We need not decide precisely which one here.

The second important concern facing the just society is to establish who the beneficiaries of the system will be.

We have seen that as full moral agents we must honor not only other full moral agents, but also those capable of lesser forms of free will and of less complex inner lives. This need to honor the less complex beings must apply not only to our individual behavior, but to our institutions also.

Recall that when picking our future society impartially, we kept in mind our possible reappearance as mentally handicapped humans in such a society. In light of this possibility, we would select a society on their behalf also (since they cannot do it themselves). We would pick a society that protects the basic interests of the less able.

But why stop at mentally handicapped humans? Given the overlap in mental capacities between the lowest humans and the highest non-humans, must we not also pick on behalf of (at least some) non-humans? Not to do so violates the impartiality-concern that is at the heart of our selection test.

We have no good moral reason to be partial to our species here. Is it impossible for us to be chimps or cats or pigs in a next life? If we can be humans of very limited capacities next time around, what reason can there be to exclude our being non-humans of high mental capacities? There seems to be no reason, other than some sheer stipulation based on species-biases.

It follows that the fair society must extend basic protections (at least life, health, safety, some liberty) to many non-humans. These non-humans, then, must be considered as members of a broader fair community.

48
Sacredness and the just society. Part four

We have seen that the factors that call for a society that respects all humans, including the less able ones, also will call for respect to many non-humans. Non-humans must, then, be considered as members of a broader fair community.

Exactly what form the basic protections will take we need not decide here. It will not include access to public university education. But it will obviously include a ban on their being used as mere tools or resources.

Thus, in a just society many (if not all) animal species will not be used for human food, nor as subjects for scientific research—if such research harms them.

A complete account here would also determine which animals to include in our broader community. It will certainly include dogs, pigs, and elephants. It might not include insects.

Let's recall, however, that the imaginative exercise of picking our future society only addresses what it takes for a group of individuals to treat each other *fairly*, in *institutional* ways. The exercise does not establish all our moral duties, as individuals or as groups.

Insects and plants may fall sufficiently outside the parameters of group-membership so that issues of our intra-group fairness do not apply to them. However, if they are sentient beings possessed of some inner life, however minimal, then we need to minimize the harm that our ways of life pose for them. We need to do so based on grounds of respect for beings with inner lives. (Incidentally, if plants were sentient, we should still avoid eating animals whenever possible. Eating plants directly destroys fewer plants than eating plants indirectly through transformation into animal flesh).

But this point, about the narrow scope of institutional fairness, in turn means that the right society in not merely the just society.

The right society includes more. It is a society that does what it reasonably can to avoid harming other lives in the natural world. The right society must be friendly to the natural environment, and not only because a healthy natural environment is needed to sustain humans and its higher-species cousins. The natural environment must be respected for its own sake, because it is at least partly composed of beings with inner lives.

Can a fair economic system coexist with the need to respect the wider natural environment? We have seen that even the fair and mixed economic system is based on generating wealth, and thus growth. So far, growth-oriented economic systems have produced excessive consumption, waste, and vast byproducts (like carbon monoxide and methane) that can harm the delicate planetary ecology. Predominant economies have also encouraged excessive human population growth, which compound the problems of consumption and encroachment on natural habitats. Such policies have led to large extinctions of non-human species.

It might be possible to have a mixed and fair economic system that operates within set boundaries of total consumption and waste. It might be possible to set human population limits. Just as we can impose on each other legal restrictions on daily work hours and on uses of certain chemicals, we could impose on each other "green" restrictions on consumption, waste, and population.

Accomplishing these goals faces many practical obstacles, especially on a global level. Still, these obstacles may not be insuperable. After all, a mixed economic system already permits multiple regulations of productive and consuming activities. It could, thus, call for a rapid transition toward clean energy sources and less waste. A challenge, again, is to reduce the influence of large money-players on democracies. Many huge corporations have vested interests in existing "dirty" energy and even more so in continued high-consumption. A second challenge is to democratize many poorer countries. There are other challenges.

However, there is also hope—the most "green" countries also seem to be the most Rawlsian countries! Perhaps as countries "mature" they tend to become both more fair and more green.

49

If value drives this world, why is it such a mixed bag?

After this long foray into the individual and institutional duties of full moral agents, we return now to the larger-scale topic of the just universe.

Our original objective was to seek for the likely purpose of it all. What we have found has leaned heavily upon value. A world that has conscious beings—each of whom can feel, act, and be autonomous—has value. A world with items of unique beauty and greatness has value.

These are at least some of the reasons why our world is here.

However, at this point we must pause and deal with some natural doubts.

Many of us are struck by so much anti-value in our world—pain, suffering, disappointment, fear, anxiety, reduced possibilities, injury, and death. How can this be, if value-enhancement is the world's central driving purpose? The ancient problem of evil, notoriously intractable, must be addressed!

Recall that we began by asking about our inevitable mortality, and about the seeming fragility of our existence. Why such features? Why not have, instead, a world in which accidents, disease, cruelties, and earthquakes are absent or are much more harmless or happen only to bad guys? Why do lives, human and non-human, begin in conditions of drastically unequal opportunities? Even those that begin with great promise are at times struck down with undeserved tragedies.

Why?

We are supposing that a god is playing the game of becoming both us and our fellow creatures, so as to enhance value. We are supposing also that the enlivened individuals in this imagined world are of intrinsic and even sacred value.

If inviolable and sacred, are not the individuals of this world deserving of better conditions? Couldn't the gods, in experiencing through these individuals, have set up a world yielding more net satisfaction and less awful tragedies? Wouldn't the gods simply have come up with a better world, or many better worlds?

Behind these questions there are, for all of us, immediate personal concerns. Why do I find myself in this bind—with this particular body, at this particular place and time, with these particular challenges and difficulties? More specific yet: why did my mother get a raw deal, if that is the only life she has?

The questions that challenge the value-purpose behind our world can be subdivided as follows:

  a. There is the question of *finiteness*: why death? Or why a finite life?

  b. There is the question of *precariousness*: why is this finite life so fragile and precarious, with so little agent-control? Why are failure, injury, and death permitted to come abruptly, at any moment?

  b. There is the question of *fairness*: Why is life so seemingly unfair? Why are starting conditions so unequally and randomly distributed? Why do good guys often lose and die, and bad guys flourish?

  c. There is the question of the *immensity of evil*: Why is there so much undeserved suffering and death?

We will address each in turn. The answers, if satisfactory at all, will overlap a good deal.

50
Why a finite life?

Why mortality? The answer to this ancient question is not especially difficult to see. Many have offered it. Our lives are finite so that we can live them with urgency and zest. Knowing that we will soon die adds preciousness and immediacy to our conscious existence.

Imagine that one's earthly life had no end. After some significant time of the same life, such as eight hundred years, one would tire of it. After being more or less the same type of person in the same type of world-context—changes notwithstanding—experience will lose some of its luster and of its capacity for wonder and surprise. One would begin to think that there is nothing new under the sun. This weariness will set in at different rates, but eventually each of us would feel it. This would be particularly so if the danger of dying from other causes—life's precariousness—were removed.

A single personality living in a world of no time-limits would eventually lose its zest for life.

Nonetheless, it is fair to wonder if an infinite life wouldn't be preferable to a complete stoppage of existence. Would we not all trade death for a diminishment of life-zest and immediacy?

Naturally, we need not imagine, as did Swift, an immortal life that involves further and further physical and mental decay. Swift was assuming current life-conditions, which feature continuous aging.

Our big question is more fundamental. Why couldn't a value-driven god have come up with different life-conditions? A god surely could have. So, why did this god not imagine a life where individuals reach their prime and then simply remain at that level forever or for as long as they choose?

Practical difficulties, like the overpopulation of our planet, cannot be the barriers to this possibility. These practical difficulties could easily have been fixed. An earth could have been made that gradually expands. Other planets could have been made accessible to us. A different setting altogether could have been imagined, where the curious act of having children is not featured. Our number could have been more fixed. The possibilities abound.

Would such different and infinite life-conditions bring inevitable loss of felt luster and immediacy to participants? If one knows that one will live forever, would the urgency to accomplish anything now, to enjoy anything now, to help someone now, evaporate? Would we become perpetual procrastinators?

These are serious concerns.

We could be in a world where we are each the super young and healthy and accomplished princes and princesses we mentioned earlier, the ones who feel perpetual self-sufficient contentment. Yes, this princely contentment would not preclude our inventing and playing new games, or creating new music. But would this state permanently satisfy us?

We have good reasons for thinking otherwise.

In a world of immortality and permanent contentment the sense of drama and adventure would cease, or greatly diminish. Even the joys of game-playing would diminish, since wins and losses would have little significance. So what if one loses! There are infinite other chances to win in the future. The joy of new music would diminish. There is an infinite stream of music still to come later. Entire genres of music premised on losses and fear and trepidation would have little appeal. All losses could be made up. Would love have much meaning in this context of no finality? Family, after all, would last forever and lovers either can't be lost or are always replaceable.

Might we, in a setting of immortality and contentment, be prompted to invent dramatic games with real dangers? Would we have to reconvince ourselves that these more potent games carry real and final dangers? Would we basically not reintroduce our current life-conditions, to restore drama and zest?

51
Why a finite life? Part two

We have seen that ordinary immortality brings with it loss of zest. Yet we would not want to trade immortality for a more zestful but limited life.

What we *really* want is a form of immortality that makes room for real drama and danger. That is the simple and natural answer!

We need an immortal life with episodes during which we forget our permanent safety and good-fortune. These might be episodes involving dramatic romance-games, where rejection and loss would really hurt. They might be games and challenges where failure, injury, and even death are seen as real possibilities.

We want immortality infused with genuinely dramatic episodes, genuine perils, genuine accomplishments, captivating art.

We basically want immortality combined with our current (perceived) precarious life-conditions!

Can we stretch our current life-conditions to make them last forever? Perhaps if we were immortal, we could avoid life-weariness by periodic fresh starts. We could change our lives every fifty or one hundred years, by moving elsewhere and remaking our lives with new friends and new professions. We could, thus, construct new lives for ourselves, and keep going, and then do it again in one hundred years.

However, what might happen after going through many of these life-changes for centuries?

Would we carry the memories of our former lives with us? Might these memories make the later lives heavy with nostalgia, guilt, sadness, in light of past tragedies? Might we get tired of being with ourselves?

What would past tragedies even be, if everyone lived forever, only changing?

Even if our bodies were to stop aging at our physical prime, might we get tired of them? Would we have to make recourse periodically to plastic surgeons to revise our looks? Would we have to make recourse periodically to psychic surgeons to revise the feel of our inner lives? Might we, even so, eventually get tired of being ourselves and of this particular endless game?

It would seem that weariness will inevitably take root. Like the speaker of Ecclesiastes, we would not see anything really new under the sun.

We would notice the recurrence of similar patterns of accomplishments, of friends-formation, of friends-loss, of skills-development. These patterns would become predictable. We would gradually lose the enthusiasm for these recurrent dramas.

How about a new wrinkle? How about an infinite life with memory breaks?

What if there were indeed psychic surgeons—or at least brain ones—that could enable us to forget many or even all of our former life-parts? What if with each new life-phase we forget our past family, place, accomplishments, friends, skills, and aspirations? *Then* our enthusiasm for the dramatic game would be renewed. It would be renewed because life would feel fresh, as if happening for the first time.

This looks to be the kind of thing we want! We need infinite life combined with the feel of fresh inner lives.

52
Combining finiteness and immortality

We have seen that the ideal combination is an immortal life mixed with periodic episodes of psychic renewals. We want to keep re-experiencing life as if for the first time. Variety, zest, and drama, will be central to this revised form of immortality.

What we want is an infinite life, but broken in segments. The segments of life would be separated by forgetfulness. One would, in effect, live many lives.

What about bodily continuity? Can each of these life-segments begin as if anew, having forgotten past life-segments, while inheriting a used body?

Let's even assume a context where everyone periodically engages in psychic surgery and forgetfulness. No one would recognize themselves or others. No one could then be a reminder of one's own past family and profession and accomplishments.

We can even assume that, in addition to the psychic surgery, everyone gets relocated to different climates and geographies to enhance their felt sense of novelty.

Could these kinds of scenarios of bodily immortality permit one to inherit a grown body while feeling like a new person?

They could, if pressed far enough.

One must not feel as if one is inheriting someone else's body, even if it were in good condition. One must not inherit the hands of a sculptor or of a farmer while now seeking to be a violinist.

To complete the refreshing process we can push the science fiction scenario further, and permit radical body rejuvenation. This would enable each later life-segment, each new persona, to feel as if they are starting life early, perhaps at the age of twelve, or perhaps even younger.

The upshot is that such an enhanced futuristic possibility is one way of periodically restoring freshness and enthusiasm into an infinite life.

Once we add for each self-contained persona the sense of mortality, the sense that he or she will cease unexpectedly at some foreseeable point, we will have reconstructed the feel of our own lives.

Why was not the world set up this way? Surely if we can easily imagine such a world, it would have been even easier for the gods to imagine it. It would have been for them an instantaneous recognition. So, why did the gods not produce this alternate world instead?

There is, again, a natural answer! The option of an infinite yet always fresh and segmented life has not only been available to the gods all along, but it has been our reality all along! Many of us have simply refused to see it!

Yes, we are talking about some form of reincarnation. We are probably living in this type of world right now! There is, after all, very little difference between body rejuvenation and new bodies!

53
Combining finiteness and immortality. Part two

We have seen that the logic of the combined needs for life-zest and for immortality calls for some form of reincarnation. The gods would have glimpsed this immediately.

This means that our existence has probably always been infinite, and broken into finite parts separated by forgetfulness. Each of the life-parts has really felt like a fresh start, because one starts off with a new body, a new psychic make-up, and a new world-setting.

The producer of this scenario is not futuristic science. It is the natural mechanics of the universe as envisaged by sensible gods.

While most of us in the west have looked askance on this possibility, many in other major traditions, particularly Hindu and Buddhist ones, have taken it as natural.

The reincarnation-scheme fits nicely as an answer to the above concerns about finiteness. It has the natural fit of an old shoe. We must not be ultimately finite. Yet life must feel as though it were finite. If it did not, it would feel less dramatic and precious.

Most importantly, this answer fits with our deep intuitions about *fairness*. If we were really finite, and this is the only life we had, life would be deeply unfair. Even if future science could produce the kind of artificial immortality for future people that we envisaged earlier, what about current and past people?

A reincarnation scheme is needed for the fair treatment of all people of all times. It would, of course, also be needed for the fair treatment of non-human animals.

It is true that the actual evidence for reincarnation is not decisive. However, there may be more evidence than we think.

Most of us know people who report having flashes of seemingly different lives. Researchers like Ian Stevenson have carefully investigated the veracity of some past-life claims, often claims made by children. Their findings are suggestive. Tibetan priestly Lamas regularly start off as children who pick out, among sets of objects, those objects associated with the recently deceased Lama. The Mozart-type phenomena of child geniuses might only be explainable through past lives.

While this evidence may not be decisive, we must be careful. Here, too, our physicalist tendencies together with western religious dogmas may blind us to such evidence. Western religious dogmas have almost certainly blinded us to the obvious fairness of reincarnation schemes.

We must also keep in mind that the logic of a reincarnation scheme itself may account for the uncertainty of the evidence in its favor. If evidence of our past lives were more extensive and continuous, perhaps through common memories of our past lives, such evidence would diminish our zest for this life. Past-lives memories would bleed into this life, with the traumas and sadness of these other lives. Past-life memories and feelings would interfere with each life having the fresh inner feel of a first life.

In any case, the central point for our big picture is that a reincarnation scheme has a better shot at being cosmically fair than any other scheme. It is best equipped to be fair to individuals who carry value and sacredness.

This promise of fairness allows a reincarnation scheme to partner happily with a cosmic scheme driven by value, and to partner particularly well with a scheme driven by the sacred value of individuals.

We will return later to issues of cosmic respect for individuals, and of overall fairness.

54
Why is this finite life so fragile and precarious?

We have seen that felt preciousness and immediacy and drama add value to an existence. A keen sense of finiteness may be necessary for such value.

What about precariousness? Does a sense that one could suddenly lose the things one most values also contribute to the immediacy-value?

To see that this is so, let's imagine the opposite. Let's suppose a scenario of full control.

If one controlled the big outcomes in our lives—time and manner of death, of major losses and accomplishments, of major failures, of major health problems—one's life would become impoverished. The felt intensities of one's accomplishments and successes would diminish.

If one knows one is going to win a tennis game, perhaps because the opponent is clearly inferior, then one's level of excitement, alertness, and participation in the game almost inevitably diminishes.

Note how even when watching on TV, live events are more compelling than taped versions of that same events where the winning outcome is guaranteed. The uncertainties of the live events make them more engaging.

This principle applies also to our bigger games involving love, career, health, and longevity. If one knows in advance that the person of your love-dreams will love you back, or will not stop loving you, one will generally value it less. The preciousness of love rests precisely on the other's spontaneity, not on one's own control.

A sense of the fragility and precariousness of one's life, and of others' lives, will prompt us to take each other's lives and accomplishments more seriously. Precariousness, like finiteness, is needed for the felt preciousness and excitement of living.

Precariousness adds drama, even if it leads to outcomes that are at times heart-rending.

This precariousness, of course, must not be final or ultimate. If it were, the added excitement and preciousness of life would be purchased at too high a price. The price would be ultimate loss and unfairness.

If some succeed and some fail, some get cancer some don't, some find or lose love partners, some don't—and if all these outcomes occur somewhat uncontrollably, and often irrespective of performance, then there better be more for each living being than this current life.

Temporary unfairness we can take, if hiding behind it is both justification and compensation. Ultimate unfairness cannot be a feature of a world that is both governed by value-enhancement and that contains individuals of independent value.

What is of great value must be treated as such. If we (humans or not) are of great value, then we must be treated with fairness. We are of great value, and hence we deserve to belong to a fair world. Surely the value-driven forces behind the structure of this world are capable of such fairness!

Again, the possibility of an infinite existence broken into seemingly separate lives feels like the right answer. A lived drama in which one is fully immersed may end unexpectedly early. But if one has other dramas, these abrupt ends are not ultimate. Other dramas may include circumstances where one lives a long life.

Similar points can be made regarding health, love, fame, power, wealth. Winners and losers can exchange roles in other lives. Balance and justice can be restored.

55
Why is life seemingly unfair?

Let us say more about this central topic of fairness, since we have been appealing to it multiple times.

Fairness means getting as one deserves. In group treatment, it also means that equals should be treated equally, and unequals should be treated unequally. For instance, those who perform equally on exams usually deserve and equal grade. Two implications are that good guys deserve good rewards, and that beings of equal value deserve equal opportunities.

Most if not all of us have an innate recognition of fairness. Our anger, as Plato noted, generally signals a perceived unfairness. Many non-humans also share this sense of fairness, as recent studies with capuchin monkeys have shown. Their anger also signals some perceived unfair distribution of rewards.

On the face of it our lives are not fair. The good guys who perform well morally are not always rewarded. In a similar way, opportunities among humans, as well as among elephants and others, are vastly unequal.

Some of this unfairness is connected, as we have seen, with the precariousness of life. For life to feel fully precious, for it to feel urgent and dramatic, it must occasionally be subject to seemingly sudden and unpredictable failures and stoppages. Such failures and stoppages, to be really unpredictable, must happen both to the brave and to the scoundrels. Some losses must, thus, appear undeserved.

This is the beginning of an answer to the perennial question: why do bad things happen to good people?

Let's explore this answer some more.

Consider the possibility of a world in which abrupt life failures and stoppages only happened to scoundrels. We would, of course, quickly figure this out, and simply avoid becoming scoundrels. For, no one wants cancer and premature death.

However, in such a world we would learn to avoid becoming scoundrels for the wrong reasons. We would be tempted to be good only to serve our personal interests. At a minimum, our moral motivation would be marred. It is even likely that our outward moral virtue would become completely phony in such a world.

If moral virtue and full moral responsibility—tied to our reflective free will—are of value, then success must not be guaranteed to the braves.

Since moral virtue is an important value (a strange but real value nonetheless), the braves must at times lose. Moral virtue needs a context of uncertainty of rewards.

This uncertainty must at least apply to the short term rewards of our current life.

The uncertainty of rewards might also have to apply to after-life settings. We must not know in advance that a paradise awaits those who are the braves. This knowledge might make paradise the main reason for good deeds. If attaining paradise were the main motive prompting agents to be good, such goodness would diminish in moral significance.

One gets moral points not merely for doing good deeds, but for doing these deeds because one recognizes that self and others count alike, and count intrinsically. Virtue requires honoring others because they deserve to be honored, not because one is looking for moral points or for happiness or for paradise.

At a minimum, moral virtue needs uncertainty of earthly rewards for the moral agent involved. This helps to explain why some good guys lose and die, and why some bad guys flourish and survive.

Naturally, as we have seen, if this unfairness were final, with no other chances or compensations, it would be too steep a price for the purchase of genuine moral accomplishments. Thus, life needs after-life continuation, in the interest of final balance and justice. A multi-lives scheme would fit this bill.

56
Why is life seemingly unfair? Part two

We have seen how the need for genuine moral virtue helps to explain one sort of unfairness: why bad things happen to good people.

Unfortunately this only addresses the needs of, and for, mature moral agents. The world, however, contains more than mature moral agents and their needs. Irrevocable calamities also occur to non-moral agents such as children and animals.

Consider the seemingly unfair distribution of initial life-conditions for innocents, such as children.

Children in our world are born with vast disparities in potentials and possibilities. Some are born talented and in fortunate contexts. For these there are plenty of opportunities for achievement and satisfaction. Other children start off deprived and diseased. Millions are born in desperate and dangerous slums. For these less fortunate, suffering and deprivation, if not early death, are the likely prospects.

These vast initial disparities cannot be morally explained if children are new creations. Children's fortunate and unfortunate life-beginnings cannot be the earned outcomes of their prior moral accomplishments and lapses.

Furthermore, these initial disparities cannot be explained as calamities necessary for the moral virtue of these same children, since children are not yet capable of such virtue. Some will never become capable, due to early deaths. Others who are deprived and abused face great obstacles to attaining virtue, since they are forced to operate at desperate survival levels. They are more likely to carry deep anger than more fortunate children, and hence more prone to do harm.

The same can be said for non-human animals. They also start off with vast disparities of prospects. Even if some animals can attain minimal levels of moral virtue, many never make it alive to reach this phase.

A multi-lives scheme gives us the best chance for fairness here.

A child who gets no real chance in this life—one who gets a sickly, painful life and dies at the age of two—will get better chances in other lives. If this is the only life this child gets, this precious individual would have been dishonored by a value-driven universe.

Moreover, there is a chance that the whole individual, of whom this child's life is a segment, has invited this tough life because of past misbehavior freely chosen, or because of some past unbalanced perspective. The chance of a deprived life serving the needs of "the individual" rests on the possibility of more fortunate lives.

A difficult life (that one has not currently brought on oneself) might be a necessary form of tough love. Tough love at times must let the individual touch bottom, as the only way to learn difficult lessons. Some may want to call this form of tough love the cosmic law of Karma. But it could also be a form of self-love.

A multi-lives scheme allows for many possibilities here. A difficult life might be selected in advance, in a pre-life setting. It might be selected in an outside-of-time setting.

The general point is that a just and compassionate universe would give an individual more than one chance. A person, or an animal, that gets no real chance in life should get other chances if the world is to be fair. At the very least, one must have gotten other chances already. Even a person who messes up badly in one life, despite good opportunities, should probably get other chances.

The disparities in initial possibilities among the creatures all around us simply have no other plausible justifications.

57

Is a multiple-lives scheme itself fair?

Multiple-lives schemes must claim that they are fair to every individual. Such schemes must, however, admit that they have an unusual idea of individuals. How can the same individual own lives he or she does not typically recall? How fair is it that the light or heavy load from alien or at least forgotten lives is placed on our current shoulders? Is it fair for the current person to inherit a difficult personality, or difficult challenges, or difficult initial circumstances?

How other can (past) people count as a current person's past existences? Even if there seem to be memory connections, what possible underlying entity might one have to be in order to make sense of these connections? A soul? What is that?

We must grant that the fairness of multiple-lives schemes relies on the presence of a single underlying entity that takes many personality-forms. We could name this a soul, though the name does not matter.

Can there be an underlying soul-entity that lives fragmented existences that transmit debt or credit from one life to the other?

We have reasons to think so, so long as some memory links tying these segments together exist at some point. Such memory links could occur within or in-between lives. They could even occur at the end of the series of lives.

Could either of these possibilities—recollections in-between lives, or within a life, or at the end of the life-series—take place? There seems to be first-person *anecdotal empirical evidence* of past-lives recollections. We mentioned before the research of psychologist Ian Stevenson in this area. A recent dispassionate assessment of this research by the philosopher Robert Almeder concludes that the evidence it provides for reincarnation is at least as strong as that provided by fossils for the past existence of dinosaurs.

Psychotherapy seems to be an area where such anecdotal evidence recurs. Psychotherapists who use hypnosis as a therapy tool frequently seem to produce past lives recollections.

Even if this evidence is legitimate, and establishes some memory-links among lives, there remains the fairness issue. It is the local personality that acts and suffers in a life-segment. How fair is it for this local personality to bear the burdens and favors of past (or simply other) personas with whom it is connected?

The answer would have to be that each local personality is one manifestation of an underlying entity. It is really the underlying entity that is engaged in the multiple-role-playing. The underlying entity must be, simultaneously, both the local personality and the greater self. Does this make sense? Can we shed light on this through analogies?

We do engage in many roles during a single life journey. We play the role of child, adult, student, teacher, dancer, father, and so forth. The personality traits we display in each of these phases and roles can differ dramatically. The reformed born-again person may hardly resemble the prior hard-drinking criminal. The born-again person might even have repressed the memories of its past life-phase, because these are too painful. Yet, it would still be fair for this later person to have to repay the old victims of its prior and repressed behavior.

In similar ways a later personality might, in fairness, inherit and incur the burdens of previous (or, simply, other) personalities that have been analogously 'repressed' and generally forgotten.

The point is that recalling past deeds is unnecessary for current responsibility for these deeds. Here is another way of showing it. Let's imagine a person who, through negligent driving, kills another person and simultaneously suffers a head injury that leads to permanent loss of memory of the accident. Surely the amnesiac person would still be responsible and punishable for the earlier killing.

We must also recall why memories of other lives are not commonplace. We need the intense identification with our current circumstances that make this life so dramatic. We need the sense of a fresh start.

58

Is a multiple-lives scheme itself fair? Part two

There is another way of questioning the fairness of multiple-lives schemes. What is the point of gaining wisdom in any given life, at times through many hardships, if we are going to lose this wisdom in the interest of making a fresh start? Should we not be able to take advantage of hard-learned lessons from past lives?

The answer is that past life-lessons can be transmitted across lives in more than one way. Life-lessons can serve as factors determining some of the circumstances and challenges one faces in this life.

One's past success at handling difficult family relations in one life could explain one's current healthy family circumstances—so that one can now focus on intellectual, artistic, political, or larger social challenges.

Alternatively, one's neglect of family duties in the past could explain one's current heavy family burdens, such as having to care simultaneously for sick parents and for young and troubled children.

Generally, access to the wisdom acquired through past lives need not feel subjectively as if it came from past experiences. It is possible to retain the wisdom without remembering how this wisdom was acquired.

Some young people can be unaccountably 'wiser than their years'. The striking analogy of child-geniuses in areas like music, such as young Mozart, can be instructive. Just as such child-geniuses could possess advanced skills due to learning in past lives, so can other young people possess an unusually keen and broad sense of genuine value. These morally gifted young people need not be aware of the source of their moral sensitivity. They need not attribute this sensitivity to having lived before.

Most of us have met such morally sensitive young people. The East, in particular, is full of such wise-child stories that are often tied to dead Buddhist masters.

Of course, we have not said much about the nature of a soul-entity. We have not explained how there can be one underlying entity that lives two or more lives that do not share a body. For many philosophers, and even non-philosophers, this smacks of impossibility. Even if lives that involve many bodies can be somehow linked by memory, this does not explain the underlying metaphysics or the underlying architecture.

We have to admit that the nature of such underlying soul-entity remains obscure. We can only appeal to a basic intuition. If it makes sense for a non-physical being, whose clearest feature is consciousness, to take on a bodily form at all—something admittedly mysterious— there is no reason why this same non-physical being cannot do it twice.

Does it make sense for a non-physical being, whose clearest feature is consciousness, to take on a bodily form at all? The real task lies in comprehending this. Is the idea of a non-physical being, whose clearest feature is consciousness, itself clear and real enough?

Fortunately here we have the experiences of many people who experience leaving their bodies behind for a time. For instance, near-death experiences are reported by thousands, and have been much discussed recently. The experiences often include a disembodied phase, when that person's body is seen from above.

Such experiences help us to at least form an idea of a non-embodied conscious personality. An entity that can apparently leave its physical body, yet retain its full consciousness, is the kind of entity that could in principle take on more than one body. A soul-entity might be this kind of thing.

Naturally, unusual experiences like near-death experiences can be denied, or explained away as hallucinations. However, the NDE data is very extensive, and it sports many common features. The impact it has on many of those who have NDE experiences is often deep and lasting, unlike the impact of hallucinations. At some point skepticism can be excessive and dogmatic.

59
Is a multiple-lives scheme the best one?

Humans have long had the visceral feeling that having a single, finite, and precarious life is an unfair arrangement. Probably as soon as humans became capable of reflection they began to rage against this. Ancient epics like that of Gilgamesh may attest to this.

Thus, many traditions have adopted after-life cosmic schemes that address this unfairness. They have not all turned to reincarnation for solutions. Why not adopt one of these other after-life schemes that do not rely on more than one life? The answer is that these other after-life schemes fall short of fairness.

The most popular alternatives, of course, appeal to after-life compensation. The basic idea is that the unfairness suffered by individuals in their one life is rectified after death through some system of reward and punishment—a Heaven, Hell, Purgatory system.

Can some after-life system of this type, attached to a single earthly life, make everything fair? These schemes have the virtue of making an individual's existence infinite. However, there are deep moral problems with these types of after-life schemes.

First, there is the issue of proportionality between deeds and punishments. If Peter is a serious scoundrel in his single life, does he go to a permanent Hell? No, infinite punishment in return for very finite misbehavior cannot be right.

Suppose, instead, that we reduce the infinity of the punishment. We could do this in two ways.

One way would be for Hell to consist of some temporary punishment or torture. Suppose Peter, the scoundrel, pays for the misdeeds through a finite period of passive suffering in a temporary Hell. Suppose that at the end of this suffering period Peter advances to a permanent Heaven, together with everyone else.

This would indeed make the scheme more compassionate. It would, however, greatly reduce the significance of moral behavior in this life, contrary to typical presuppositions of moralistic Abrahamic systems. Moral virtue would be of diminished value because it would no longer be required for heaven. In fact, why have our current type of life, with its complex scheme of free will, randomness, and undeserved suffering in the first place, if performance merely hastens one's ascent to heaven?

Suppose that Peter, the scoundrel, is morally retested in a purgatory setting, before he finds a permanent placement in an everlasting Hell or Heaven. Would this revision fix the problem?

This might fix the issue of proportionality between crimes and punishments, but at the cost of abandoning the one-life-only scheme. Consider what a purgatory setting must be like to permit morally valid retesting. This setting will look like a second life. Recall that a valid setting for moral testing would require similar conditions to the ones that we face here. If not, such retesting would not be fair to the rest of us who have to pass the tests in our current life. The purgatory-Peter, then, would have to have free will, which he could use well or badly. He would have to face a world that is equipped with the same degree of haphazard and precarious rewards as in our current life. He must not know that the virtuous always win. He must have a mortal body-form of the same level of fragility and precariousness as ours. Only so will his good deeds carry genuine moral worth.

The more conditions we place in this second post-life existence, to make it morally comparable to our life, the more it looks like Peter is simply having a second life. But, then, this fair purgatory system would really constitute a two-lives reincarnation scheme. The fact that this second life would occur in a non-earth setting would not matter, so long as the action-conditions are the same.

Moreover, suppose that Peter only gets these two mortal lives. Suppose he is a scoundrel in both lives. Does he now deserve the infinite torture of Hell? Again, very finite misbehavior cannot deserve infinite punishment. The previous problem resurfaces again.

60
Child tragedies and one-life compensatory schemes

Consider, also, the difficult issue of children's initial and unearned misfortunes —ones that lead to early childhood death. Can after-life compensations appealing to typical Heaven-Purgatory-Hell scenarios rectify these children's tragic misfortunes?

It is difficult to see how. The basic problem is that attempts to compensate the initial unlucky ones, in an afterlife realm, would generate new unfairness. Recall that fairness requires that equals be treated equally. All children are of equal worth or status. Fairness requires equal opportunities and equitable rewards for them.

Why would attempts to compensate the initial unlucky ones in an afterlife realm create further unfairness?

Consider some well-known possible schemes of compensation.

Suppose the deprived innocent child who dies young is sent directly to a permanent heaven. This would unfairly penalize those of us who can attain this heaven only by passing moral tests. The children sent directly to a permanent heaven did not have to pass such moral tests. Since these tests are super-risky—failure results in everlasting punishments—it follows that the children who suffer and die early become the long-term *undeservedly lucky* ones. They are guaranteed heaven simply by being born deprived.

Suppose that, like Peter, these children are first morally retested in a purgatory setting, before ascending to heaven. Again, for this retesting to be valid and comparable to ours, the after-life setting would have to replicate our kind of precarious world. The requisite after-life setting would have to be a second life. This revised scheme would then be a reincarnation scheme in all but name.

Suppose everyone upon death moves directly to heaven—innocents and guilty alike. If so, life would be unfair to those morally virtuous ones who have proven themselves. These latter have made the right choices in life, have passed the moral tests. In doing so, they have at times sacrificed desired earthly advantages and benefits. Selfish and cruel people have done the opposite. If all get the same reward, the scheme would be both unfair and dishonoring of moral accomplishments.

We should trust our common sense regarding fairness here.

We must insist that a universe aiming at value would prize and respect the well-being of sacred individuals. It would value their suffering and undeserved losses. It would honor their free will and accomplishments, including moral ones. These individuals should get respect and fair treatment. Fair treatment by the universe consists of equals being treated equally, and of unequals being treated unequally.

It is simply hard to see how everyone can be treated fairly in after-life schemes like the Christian and Islamic ones. The doctrine of everlasting Hellish torment, held by these traditions, is especially unfair.

We have briefly alluded to scenarios involving finite after-life heavens and hells. Could these make one-life schemes fair? These scenarios would at least not face the proportionality problem that infinite rewards and punishments have. However, these scenarios have to deal with the mortality issue. What happens to us after the temporary after-life state? Do we all cease to be? That brings back the problems with mortality we discussed earlier. Do we get reabsorbed in an impersonal divine being? Such absorption would imply the loss of separate individuality. It would amount to a personal death. Is individuality not worthy and sacred?

Besides, in such temporary after-life schemes, the child who did not really get a shot at the unique accomplishments of this life would remain deprived. Typical passive conceptions of heaven, where the individual can enjoy but can no longer fail or succeed (at least at moral and dramatic tasks), cannot make up for the dramatic *agency* of this life. If, alternatively, a heaven is as active and risky as life, then it becomes a second life. Temporary heavens and hells only make sense within multiple-lives schemes.

61

Is a multiple-lives scheme the best one? Part two

We have, thus, seen some moral problems with attempts to make one-life schemes right by means of after-life compensations.

Are there other ways to make one-life schemes right without appealing to after-lives?

It does not look like it. Bad things happening to good people, and the reverse, are features of life that cannot be made right within the resources of a single life.

What about the system-level need for haphazard rewards that, we have seen, is necessary for genuine virtue? Can't this factor, alone, account for the bad things that happen to good people? We have granted that deadly cancers and accidents must occur to some good people, so that others will be properly tested. The test is to see if people do the right thing for its own sake, knowing that doing right will not significantly improve their chances at longevity, health, and happiness—or that of one's loved ones. Must some not be sacrificed for this noble purpose of making possible moral virtue and compassion?

Many are initially attracted to this view. However, if this view presumes a single-life context, then it becomes morally abhorrent. The value and sacredness of individuals bars their being used merely for the nobility of others—without some compensation to the innocent victim. Even with compensation-schemes there might be moral problems... unless one somehow signs up for the risks of victimization. Joe cannot abuse Ed against Ed's will on the grounds that Joe, or some divine third party, will make it up to Ed later.

Without such compensations-schemes things are even worse. The use of some for the possible virtue of others treats the victims as tools. Individuals with inner lives cannot be treated as mere tools.

Had the victims volunteered to be violated, it would be a different matter. However, we do not normally volunteer for child-abuse, cancer, or for serious accidents. (There are multi-lives schemes where, for reasons of balancing for past privileged points of view or for past mistakes, people are said to invite disastrous circumstances in a given life.)

A similar response should be given to the proposal that a child's unearned disability and misery might be the parents' fault. Might the parents have misbehaved, thus transmitting flaws, diseases, deprivations to their children? Might we view life in terms of family units, instead of treating individuals as atomic and independent?

This type of answer will not do. Each inner life counts and is inviolable, whether inside or outside family contexts. Thus, it is morally unfair for children to have to carry their parents' debts or sins, since children had no role in acquiring such debts and sins. Second, children are not always born handicapped or diseased through some fault of the parents. Third, some parents attain their misfortunes undeservedly; and other parents acquire their fortunate position (one that favors their children) through evil means. In both of these last two cases the disadvantages and advantages inherited by the respective children would be undeserved.

Might we view life in terms of species units, permitting the sins of the species' first parents—such as Adam and Eve, for example—to be transmitted to all descendents? Might it be that no child comes in the world innocent, due to this original sin?

Clearly this is an insane notion. Cultures periodically invent such notions. Loading a new child, an alleged new creation, with some primordial grandparents' sins or sinfulness dishonors the child. It pains to see that for centuries many of us have accepted this notion.

The invention of the doctrine of an original sin afflicting all humans is instructive, however. It reveals how desperately far we might go in attempts to make one-life schemes seem fair.

The conclusion is that if we care about fairness, the right thing to do is to abandon one-life views.

62

Is a multiple-lives scheme the best one? Part three

Are there yet other ways to make one-life schemes right without appealing to afterlives?

Can the big-picture need for variety in life-circumstances provide an explanation for undeserved ills? Might individuals simply have to start off with unexplained disadvantages, for the sake of an overall mosaic of life? Might this mosaic be one where the elements are individuals of different capacities, of widely varied life-beginnings, and of different in-life calamities? Might the variety of individuals needed for the mosaic have to include seriously sick and deprived children with no chance at fulfillment?

This cannot be. Life is not primarily a giant composite aiming at some aesthetic big-picture goal. It is primarily not a mosaic made up of disposable individuals. Life is lived by individuals.

There may well be big-picture goals for the universe, such as our current proposal's value-enhancement purpose. However, big-picture goals must not violate individuals who possess their own independent value-status and agency. The expanding totality of value-enhancement— if we are right—is attained *through* the lived experiences and doings of sacred individuals

Each inner life counts and is inviolable.

Variety and mosaics of life may carry some independent value at the composite level. Again, though, such composite-level value must not violate individuals. Even if there were a mass-mind consciousness at some level above that of individual minds, such a mass-mind could not exist at the expense of individuals.

Larger life-mosaics are like nations. Their reality depends on the reality of individuals, not the reverse.

If individuals are sacred, they cannot be used as mere tools for some larger purpose. A just universe could not permit this. Any legitimate divine plan could not be based on this.

There is a general lesson to be drawn here. We have seen that fair treatment of humans and animals—as individuals—looks to be impossible within the confines of single-life schemes.

In addition, we have seen that if there is a distinctive and shared purpose for individuals of the human species—and a purpose tied to human accomplishments here on earth—then such accomplishment-related purpose cannot be achieved well in a single life.

Is there such a purpose?

63

Is moral accomplishment the unique human purpose?

We have seen that our very existence enhances value. It does so through our inner lives, through inner happiness and varieties of feelings and emotion, through our dramatic and intense and unpredictable adventures.

Each life is unique. A life of deep devotion to another person, or to a group cause, or to the study of ancient manuscripts, or to new architectural forms, adds to the ultimate value of the universe. Even a life of shallow and scattered devotions adds something unique to this value-collection.

However, we have seen that accomplishments also count. An experience-machine, or many of these, could reproduce exact duplicates of our unique, unpredictable, and varied inner lives. An experience machine could duplicate the mosaic level of varied consciousnesses, and could even duplicate phony accomplishments. Yet it would leave out the agency aspect and its genuine accomplishments.

Of course, the agency aspect with its genuine accomplishments applies to non-human animals too. They must also not be replaceable by experience-machine counterparts.

Is there something about our own agency and accomplishments that is especially unique, and that can point at a uniquely human purpose?

Obviously, our specialty is possession of an advanced and reflective imagination that leads to the possibility of autonomous free will. These capacities make the range and level of our accomplishments immensely larger when compared to the accomplishments of other known creatures.

We can build cathedrals, planes, and weird systems of thought. We can reshape our world, both the outer environment and the inner character, in radical ways.

We have seen that our kind of advanced free will extends the unpredictability of our life-stories to the inner character realm. Advanced free will makes us ultimate part-authors of our inner script. We do not simply act out our role the way animals do, expressing our unpredictable agency only when external circumstances dictate (like the presence of multiple foods, or of multiple scents). We can help to redefine the very role we are initially given as we go along.

We can decide which inclinations we are going to promote and develop. We can decide to ignore or gradually remove our desire for smoking, or for meat, or for money, or even for safety and survival.

Might this special capacity for self-shaping characters—more than our capacity for external accomplishments like cathedrals, planes, and theoretical physics—point at uniquely human purposes?

One such unique purpose is the moral responsibility for the course of our lives. We co-write our lives, and hence we carry a lot more responsibility for the actions and outcomes of our lives. This self-shaping capacity has a bearing on how we treat ourselves and others— humans, non-humans, and nature. It has a bearing on our individual acts of kindness, compassion, and what is sometimes called spirituality. It has a bearing on the group institutions we construct, and whether these honor humans, non-humans, and nature.

We are the only species that can score full and genuine moral points.

Perhaps learning to handle such awesome moral responsibility is the uniquely human purpose.

This latter proposal has been advanced by many thinkers and traditions. Is the attainment of moral virtue, then, our species' distinctive goal?

64
Moral accomplishments and many lives: the multiple chances issue

Is moral virtue, as enabled by our reflective free will, our species' distinctive goal? Important figures in ethics like Emmanuel Kant have thought so.

We must agree that moral virtue is one important human goal— at least for those humans who are able. We have seen that making possible moral virtue is one explanation for bad things happening to good people.

Is moral virtue our central or even our only distinctive goal?

We will argue later that it is not our central or only goal.

First, however, we will note that if moral virtue were the central goal of our earthly existence, this goal fits more nicely with a many-lives setting than with a single-life setting. Only in a many-lives setting can moral virtue be pursued by humans in a way that honors all individual humans. Only in such a setting can moral virtue be open to all in a fair way.

Why is this?

If our main purpose were moral virtue, this would imply that our aim is to learn to properly respect beings of intrinsic worth—beginning with ourselves, but extending to other humans, and then to other beings with inner lives. Such respect consists minimally in not harming worthy beings needlessly. Respecting others might involve also going out of one's way to help them, particularly those others who are in trouble and innocent and unable to help themselves.

Can we truly learn to properly respect self and others in a single life? The answer is no, for both obvious and deep reasons.

The obvious reason is that a single opportunity is subject to too many arbitrary limitations, as we have seen. We do not all get an equal chance to accomplish moral and spiritual goals within a single life. Some get no chance at all. Infant death, for instance, permits no opportunity for moral virtue for the infant that dies.

Even for adult humans, unchosen psychological and cultural handicaps make it a lot more difficult for some to learn to respect themselves and others in a principled and consistent way. Having multiple lives would widen these opportunities, and might equalize them.

Some adult humans are fortunate to face moral tests without major handicaps. Yet even for these humans, having more than one life through which to prepare for these tests, or to learn from mistakes, would be a fairer method of testing. Multiple trials and errors are generally needed to learn complex lessons. We tend to learn in phases. This applies whether we are learning math or carpentry or tennis.

We must note, sadly, that many of us fortunate adults, with full moral capacities, living in the richer communities of the world, are still engaged in morally dishonorable behavior. Note the prevalence of spouse or child abuse, the willingness to tolerate killing and being killed in wars of dubious reasons, and the prevalence of treating sentient animals as if they were our tools.

While these shortcomings could be simple moral failures, they suggest that either moral virtue is a tough task, or that we are obtuse.

In either case one single life is insufficient for the task of moral education to be completed. It seems insufficient even for most fortunate humans.

65
Moral accomplishments and many lives: fair and genuine testing

There is a deeper reason why a single life is not sufficient to complete our moral education—even if the distinctive purpose for human lives were moral schooling. This has to do with the nature of a complete and valid moral education.

To receive a valid moral degree from the school of life one needs to face and pass tests in a significant variety of settings. A variety of test-settings makes for more valid scores. A similar process is involved to mastering other complex skills. One must demonstrates experience and success in multiple circumstances.

Take the game of tennis.

To have mastered tennis sufficiently—to be a master tennis player—means that one has played and won on different courts, against different types of opponents, on on-days and on off-days, indoors and out-doors, etc.

Any mediocre player can play unexpectedly well on a single occasion.

Mastering the moral game of respecting others is similar.

Genuine respect for others includes non-harming (and possibly helping) others on good days—when one finds oneself in fortunate inner and outward life-circumstances.

It is easy to be kind and helpful if one has an unusually kind disposition, and while facing favorable outward circumstances (such as having nice parents, mind-expanding teachers, and good health). If we have a kind heart and are exposed to a cultural education that encourages respect for sentient beings of all species, most of us would turn out to be super good.

However, would we be equally sensitive to others if we faced more troubled inner and outward circumstances? What if one of us had grown up love-deprived, or physically-deprived—and consequently had to face chronic feelings of unworthiness, insecurity, jealousy?

What if one of us had grown up sickly and unattractive? What if one had grown up or in a culture that honors violence, or in a racist one, or in one that views all other animals as mere resources?

What if one of us is a person with strong internal urges for narcotics, or for power, or for eccentric sexuality? What if one has suffered difficult tragedies?

Would we, in unfavorable circumstances such as these, still honor others consistently? Would we still honor those outside our group? Would we honor non-humans? Would we listen to our inner voice that recognizes worthiness where our culture suggests otherwise?

To truly master a moral education that respects self and others we need to encounter at least a significant variety of these challenges. We must pass tests while equipped with varied initial motivational settings, and while facing varied outward circumstances.

In the absence of this variety of predicaments, our actual moral accomplishments might be largely a matter of luck—the result of accidentally favorable inner and outer circumstances.

A valid moral degree from the school of life needs proper testing. It needs moral challenges faced from more than one psychological and circumstantial vantage point. This requires living many lives.

66
We are here for more than moral purposes

We have seen that life as a moral school goes hand in hand with living many lives. Thus, even on a narrow moral reading of life the many-lives view is a better fit.

We also have good reasons to expand our view of life. We must notice that there is a lot more than right and wrong that counts all around us. For one thing, right and wrong behaviors imply other goods. Let's recall *why* others, both humans and non-humans, must be honored. The reasons include their having inner lives, of various levels, and their having independent agency-capacities, of various levels.

Others' lives must be respected and promoted because their being consciously alive is a treasure for them! At least, it can be!

It is not primarily to stimulate others' moral virtue that we must honor others. After all, we must also honor those capable of little or no moral virtue, like humans of limited capacities and non-human animals.

Even when it comes to fully capable humans, our honoring them has to do only partly with respecting their capacity for moral virtue. Again, their moral virtue counts only because the inner lives, the happiness, the interests, and the accomplishments of those around them matter and need to be honored.

It is because people and non-people *have worthy lives* that anyone's moral virtue matters.

They have worthy lives because of a multitude of satisfying engagements. These include close relationships and the pleasure of being with others. They also include humor, nature, music, sports, food, books, travel, building, and gardening. We saw before that these pursuits and experiences not only add subjective pleasure to our lives; they also count by enabling us to connect with things of beauty and quality.

So, we deserve to be mutually honored at least in part because of many non-moral things that count in our lives. We deserve to be honored in part because we enjoy flowers, films, sex, tennis, cathedrals, and myriad other things. We deserve to be honored also because of our uniquely human accomplishments in artistic, athletic, scholarly, and organizational areas, among others.

We cannot ignore the great cathedrals. We cannot ignore Caravaggio. The life of a painter who neglects most human relationships, and even moral virtue, for the sake of painting excellence cannot be judged a simple failure. Caravaggio may have been a troubled and violent fellow, but his astonishing art is a superior accomplishment.

These types of accomplishments cannot be mere means to moral ends; nor are they mere sideshows.

Non-moral values show that our life-schooling must aim widely. Its aims must include non-moral areas of fun, quality, and value. We must engage in, appreciate, and create within these other dimensions.

Here, then, is a more likely hypothesis: humans are conscious reflective and imaginative agents so that they may learn to appreciate, express, and master multiple values. We are here to master values ranging from the moral to the fun, aesthetic, athletic—all tied to the uniquely earthly realm.

We are here to learn to respect others.

We are here to enjoy each other's physical and emotional company.

We are here to smell the roses.

We are here also to invent and enjoy a good pizza and to invent and enjoy a good song.

67
Our uniquely human purpose

We have arrived at a likely hypothesis for the purpose of our lives.

We are here to learn to appreciate, express, and master, a variety of values—ranging from the moral to the aesthetic to the athletic, and to others unique to the earthly realm.

Our specifically human purpose, rich in reflection and imagination, might call for an even wider appreciation. Our purpose might call for appreciation of life in general, of the universe, of consciousness and imagination itself, and possibly of the ultimate imaginative source(s) behind all things.

Other beings, like non-human animals, may appreciate and create value more instinctively. Yet, the spectrum of values they appreciate and create is likely to be much narrower.

We are surely here to appreciate and create value more reflectively and more expansively.

This broad and reflective appreciation might have to aim first at our inner life and our individual uniqueness. We might be here to appreciate (reflectively and explicitly) that inward mysterious consciousness which is our home. But this appreciation would have to extend to that of others, in an ever enlarging circle. We must recognize that our pains are no worse than others' pains.

The enlarging circle of appreciation and concern—concern for the sake of *their* well being—would have to include the Chinese, the alligators, the flowers, and perhaps the oceans.

Our tasks might include coming to recognize that our consciousness is made of the same stuff as the divine. It might include coming to realize that the immense variety all around us is also made up of divine cloth, even if it takes the form of mountains and snowflakes.

We might have to come to see ourselves as vehicles through which our universe—a four dimensional exteriorized form of being—recognizes itself in a self-conscious way as special and as worthy.

Note that if the purpose of living were the mastery of a very broad spectrum of values, then the inadequacy of a single life scheme becomes even more acute. A broad mastery requires a varied, deep, and lasting experience of life—an experience only attainable by encountering life *from many different perspectives*. No one can come to fully appreciate in a single lifetime—even a fortunate lifetime—the experience of sports, of the arts, of raising children, of social organizing, of the specialness of self and universe, of our kinship with divine material..., all the while fully cultivating one's moral sensitivity.

To master earthly experiences and values widely, we would each have to live as men and as women, as rich and as poor, as gifted and as deprived, as physically inclined and as musically inclined, as socially free and as oppressed, in a desert and in a cold mountain climate, as shepherds and as scientists. Only from the combined experience of these first-person perspectives can we get a broad sense of the richness of the human earthly dimension.

We might even have to encounter earthly life from other animals' perspectives to get a fuller sense of what it is like *to live* on earth, as opposed to merely mastering *human* earthly forms. Sensory value—deep, unique, and varied—is, after all, value too. There are surely many sensory types of experiences only accessible though non-human life forms. A cat's experience of catnip, a bird's experience of flight, a bee's experience of flowers, these are merely some examples closest to our imaginative reach.

Viewed from the perspective of this broad purpose—that of mastering experiences and values widely—there is not a vast difference between gifted and deprived humans, or between typical humans and other animals. Each of us is likely to have embraced many of the more humble roles in our multi-lives existence.

68
The end-game

If mastering the large spectrum of earthly values, and thereby enriching the universe, is the reason why we are here, what happens when this has been accomplished? Even assuming, with Buddhists, that it's important for all of us, not just for some, to attain this mastery and experience, what happens once all accomplish this? What is the final end-game?

One proposed final goal is the mystical re-union with a divine source. Some even speak of our current life as a kind of dream from which we'll finally awaken to realize that we have been part of a god all along—but a god in a state of self-estrangement and ignorance.

The problem with this type of view—typically from Hindu-Buddhist traditions—is that it downplays and dishonors the significance of individuality and of individual personhood. Individual personhood is treated as a negative state of ignorance, separation, and ego. Personhood is viewed as the source of desire and suffering. The proposed solution is the return to a felt sense of permanent oneness and of non-ego.

Above all, this perspective does not explain why the ultimate deity at issue, the ultimate source, took on such negative false-sense of itself in the first place. Why take on first person points of view, if the goal is not to value and enjoy these, but to escape from these? Surely the deity in question did not become individuals in order to suffer!

A second proposed final goal is the return to an eternal communion with a god. This would be some sort of eternal loving embrace that preserves separateness between individual and the divine.

The weakness of this proposed goal lies in its dullness, as already seen. Even if communal, this blissful state is still static. This state does not do justice to our longing for the new, the exciting, the creative, the active. Supreme ultimate bliss might be internally satisfying. But, seen objectively, there would be nobler possibilities linked to free accomplishments. Our agency aspect is particularly penalized by such a state of contentment as the ultimate state.

A third possibility is for the continuation of each individual soul through new and unending adventures and growth. Individual existence would be an endless spiral. It would involve mastering one realm of being after another, in an endless progression of higher realms. Each individual soul would take countless forms and settings, some currently unimaginable. The goal here would be an endless expansion of experience.

Would this be satisfying in the absence of some final goal? Endless pursuits would do justice to our active side, to the side that likes new journeys and new experiences. Would this active goal be fair to the side that seeks peace and permanent bliss? Or must we say, with Nietzsche, that the desire for final peace and final bliss is not the noblest desire?

Perhaps both desires are valid—the one for a timeless oneness and the one for endless activity. Perhaps all along a side of us retains a partial sense of oneness with a divine source. This is the sense that countless mystics across the globe report having experienced. At the same time another side of us, the individual side, is engaged in an endless series of journeys in richer and newer realms.

This paradox involving a dual-aspect end-game parallels the paradox involving gods and temporality. In the latter case we saw that a god needs to forget its non-temporal aspect, to be a full participant in our worldly dramas—while never fully relinquishing non-temporality. In a related way, the individualized forms of a god—such as us—need to continue individual pursuits, while never fully relinquishing their non-temporal and divine place of safety or home. Our periodical returns to this home, for rest and re-charge from our journeys, might take the form of the mystical sense of oneness which would lie always within our reach.

This option is in line with our current proposal. If we are divine characters taking part in living dramas, we must also retain the link to the shared agency-source that lies behind each of our roles.

69
The horrors

Let's assume, then, that the answers regarding our existence that we have been seeking lie in mastering multiple values, having multiple lives, and engaging in endless journeys. Do these answers suffice to explain and justify the dark side of existence? Do they justify the massive natural and human-caused evils?

Why so much undeserved suffering and other forms of harm, to both humans and non-humans? What about the various horrors that have led many intelligent observers to deny the likelihood of benevolent divine sources? Recall Dostoyevsky's Ivan, from the book *The Brothers Karamazov*, who denies any benevolent god, based in part on his keen awareness of so much abuse and torture of children—he had compiled an extensive collection of newspaper accounts of child-abuses.

We note that these massive evils come in two forms: those caused by nature and those caused by humans. At the heart of each is the issue of fairness. Why do so many terrible, unspeakable, things happen to innocents (children are the clearest examples of innocents, but sentient animals must be included also).

Even morally guilty people may not deserve torturous treatment, as humans have come to appreciate over the centuries. Most humans no longer accept the torture of even the cruelest of scoundrels.

Still, the problem of abuse is particularly acute regarding innocents.

Let's take the evils caused by humans first. Is there a way of making the massive suffering and other harm of innocents, caused by human action, fair?

Again, the only hope for fairness lies in the factors we already mentioned. These are:

    a. The need to preserve autonomous free will. Free will can be misused in harmful ways.

    b. The need for precariousness, to make possible the drama and felt preciousness of life.

    c. The need for haphazard evils befalling on some good people, to make possible moral virtue.

    d. The possibility of some karmic-like restoration of balance to soul-individuals across lives

Will these factors suffice to explain human evils?

70

Massive harm to innocents caused by humans

Can the massive harm caused by humans—group enslavement, torture, massacres—be rendered somehow acceptable, perhaps even fair, by the four factors listed above? Can the needed precariousness of life, haphazard evils, karmic balance across lives, and autonomy, do the job?

Could these desirable features of life be attained through lesser kinds and quantities of harms?

Life's need of both perceived precariousness (for the sake of enhanced zest) and of haphazard evils (for the sake of moral virtue) can explain some significant harms to innocents, such as premature deaths.

It is far from clear that large-scale tragedies can be so explained. The need for conditions where we can suddenly and innocently suffer a downfall could be sufficiently demonstrated through some occasional downfalls. Why permit large-scale massacres?

The only hope for an explanation of massive harm caused by humans lies in the need for autonomy and for karmic balance.

In the case of humans, and of other beings with genuine autonomy, we have beings that help to reshape the rules of the game. Humans have some control over the kind of characters they become. They have some capacity to reflect on the beliefs that lead to their actions.

Thus, if a group of semi-autonomous beings adopts crazy beliefs, which in turn lead them to engage in massive violations, the gods cannot directly be blamed. They can only be blamed for either allowing autonomous beings at all, or for not blocking their actions at some destructive thresholds.

Given that advanced autonomy is an important good— and none of us would really choose to be without this capacity—divine sources can only be blamed for omitting action-blocking limits. Why do the gods not intervene when human acts get really ugly? Why do the gods not set up automatic stop-mechanisms whenever massive evils like holocausts are about to happen?

In a context of multi-lives schemes, one level of answer is that the restoration of some cosmic balance requires that past victimizers perhaps experience the role of group-victims in a different life.

Perhaps some large-scale evils were carried out because of some shared group-beliefs by the human group in power, in another life. Perhaps the group involved needs to learn to reassess such beliefs. Problematic past group-beliefs might have focused on perceived racial, ethnic, caste, or national, superiorities. They might have derived from shared and deeply held beliefs regarding the lower status of other groups.

We know that groups, nationalities, cultures, have in the past abused and terrorized other groups. Some of these abuses were carried out on the basis of perceived group-superiority attitudes (and of positions of power). The sense of superiority might well have been shared by virtually the entire group in question. The centuries-long enslavement of many darker-skinned Africans by lighter-skinned Europeans, racially based, is one of the clearest such examples. It is not the only one.

Perhaps beliefs about group-superiority can be so deeply engrained that the only way for perpetrators to reassess these beliefs is through a drastic method. A group-disaster experience, at the hands of other humans, and based on membership in a disliked group, might be such a drastic method.

We do know of individuals that can only begin to shake free from self-destructive habits by hitting bottom, and experiencing important losses. Perhaps this carries over to some destructive group-beliefs and habits. In extreme cases a group-level crash might be the only way to readjust the group's approach to life.

This does not explain why the gods allowed the first large-scale abuses by one group of humans over others. Why was there not some maximal threshold of abuse structurally built-in to begin with?

71
Massive harm to innocents caused by humans. Part two

We have seen that the karmic balance across lives can only explain a cosmic permission of subsequent human harms of massive scale. Why permit initial ones?

We have assumed that direct divine interventions are out of place, since the gods are not external observers, but active players, as us, in our current roles. Even so, why is the play of life not set up so that when massive bloodsheds are about to occur, the stage goes dark and icy water falls on the actors?

Perhaps the best we can do here is to point out that the world would then be radically different than it currently is. The implications of such an anti-massacre mechanism are quite large. The overall losses might offset the gains.

For one thing, we would not learn to avoid forms of group-madness by trial and error, and through freely chosen experiences. We would learn through a kind of coercion.

Imagine an alcoholic-leaning person whose arm is always blocked by a natural paralysis after each first drink. At some point this person will not even try for the second drink, but only because of a learned external limitation. Has he or she really learned the lesson regarding the destructive nature of alcoholic abuse? Probably not. We might even say that the agent's learning opportunity regarding alcohol has been preempted.

An artificial impulse-blocking mechanism would, for instance, preempt the inner and unpredictable moral wrestling of the alcoholic-leaning person. It would preempt processes of freely mastering one's destructive instincts.

This point might also apply at the group level.

In precluding some major tragedies, impulse-blocking cosmic mechanisms would preclude many major moral triumphs also. Groups, like individuals, have occasionally made huge moral leaps forward. The gender-equality recognition achieved in the latter half of the twentieth century in many parts of the world is one such major leap.

Of course, it is possible to argue that the possibility of such moral learning and moral triumphs (for the group in question) pales in worth when compared to the risks of massive abuses that accompany the possibility of triumphs.

But the issues here are not so clear. If offered in advance, would we take this trade-off? Would we, as a species of humans (or as some fully able sub-group), take the offer of a nature-induced restriction on our powers to harm, in exchange for restricting the range of our autonomy?

Our answer might be, No. We might choose autonomy, notwithstanding the accompanying risks of massive crimes and of massive punishments.

If that is a world that the participant themselves would choose, then there is no cosmic moral deficiency in the form of some missing harm-blocking threshold.

72
Natural massive harm to innocents

Can the massive harm caused by nature—hurricanes, earthquakes, asteroids, plagues—be rendered also somehow acceptable, perhaps even fair, by the three pertinent factors listed earlier? Can the needed precariousness of life, haphazard evils, and karmic balance across lives, do the job?

Again, life's precariousness and its haphazard evils can only explain some significant natural harm to innocents. What about massive natural catastrophes—like sudden hurricanes that kill tens of thousands of humans and animals? Wouldn't small and uncommon natural disasters be enough procure these necessary features for our lives?

It would seem so. Thus, the only possible way to make sense of large-scale natural tragedies is through some need for group karmic balance. Recall that human autonomy will not play a role here since the harm comes at the hands of non-human natural elements.

Might there be a need for group-scale karmic balance that can best be met by means of natural disasters?

Are there types of beliefs—perhaps about group-superiority or about species-superiority—that can only be unlearned through a group-humbling at the hands of nature?

Consider our massive and systemic abuse of non-human animals, currently carried out in a world where less cruel food options are available. This could be an ongoing example of group-violations based on widely shared hyper-superiority beliefs. Perhaps only a group-shock at the hands of nature can shake us into reassessing our long-standing views that animals are mere resources for human consumption.

Of course, these are speculative suggestions. Nonetheless, whatever the status of these suggestions, one thing is for sure. A multiple-lives scheme is the only scheme that even has a shot at justice-based explanations of such massive disasters. Any minimally just universe would require a scheme of this type.

There are other related puzzles concerning the role of animals in natural disasters. Why are non-human animals involved, as victims, in large group-disasters? Surely they are not moral agents to any significant degree. What moral lesson can they learn? What possible learning process could the millions of cows, pigs, and chickens be involved in that might explain their current, and past, abuses?

Might animals be forms, or fragments, of the underlying soul-entities that also take human forms? Might animals be aspects of "higher" beings who experiment with existence as "lower" life-forms? Might soul-entities do this to experience the simpler sensory and agency points of view they downplayed while enraptured in their other lives?

These are possibilities. If it is possible for a god to take up the perspective of simpler beings like us, while forgetting its higher powers, the same can occur at lower levels in the chain of being. Animals might be more limited life-forms many of us take for specific experiential or karmic-learning purposes.

Still, it is hard to know how to assess these suggestions. Furthermore, there are other and deeper puzzles involving animals.

Why are some animals by nature carnivorous, capable of surviving only by eating other animals? To say that it is natural is no answer. Why is nature so set up? Why do lions feed on deer, on conscious beings equipped with similar inner lives, on beings who want to continue enjoying earthly living? Why was nature not arranged so that the more complex animals only feed on plants or sunlight?

Such questions are very hard to answer in the context of a value-driven universe. All we can say here is that these are hard to answer on any world-view that recognizes the intrinsic worth of animals, and that tries to make moral sense of the universe. (The problem, of course, would not arise in an accidental universe).

We are left with only hints of possible answers when it comes to massive natural evils.

73
Epilogue

We have come to the conclusion of our fable.

We have addressed the seemingly chancy and unfair nature of human and non-human lives.

To deal with this, we have tried to imagine the ultimate reasons for the very presence of any universe—if chance and purposeless existence are to be ruled out.

Our proposal is that the entire cosmic game is a divine voluntary undertaking.

This cosmic undertaking must have been motivated by the potential for multiple values-realizations. This value-potential—which we termed-value-enhancement—must have prompted a mature divine mind into playing a cosmic game. The game consists in imagining, and then participating in, individualized and varied forms of life. In our case these conscious forms of life are set in peculiarly "external" spatial and temporal dimensions.

The sheer presence of life-forms with inner consciousnesses—because they matter—testifies to the value urge that must have led to this world.

This value urge also dictates that these forms of life escape divine control. Only an infantile god would individualize itself in merely sensory or in predictable and robotic forms. A mature god would seek self-expression through life-forms that are conscious, independent, creative, uncontrollable, and fun.

From our first-person vantage points, this cosmic urge towards value-enhancement is felt as the impulse to enjoy, create, and appreciate multiple values. The part about appreciating values deals, in part, with the need to honor others fully. Those others who embody first-person points of view and a qualitative inner life carry an intrinsic worth.

However, our being independent agents equipped with a special kind of advanced freedom, means that our consistent honoring of others is not guaranteed.

In fact, this task of freely honoring others, especially those others outside our preferred group or species, has proven a tough challenge. Fulfilling our own lives without making it more difficult for others to fulfill theirs has been a difficult balancing act.

To have a fair shot at mastering this balancing act we need more than one life, since some of us die very young. Of the survivors into adulthood, many carry too large a burden for their current lives to serve as valid tests for genuine moral learning. And even those of us fewer fortunate humans who get a decent shot at learning to honor others, while pursuing our own earthly enjoyment and fulfillment, have demonstrated the need for more than one lifetime of practice.

Thus, an eastern cosmology is needed. This needed eastern vision must feature: (1) the world as a divine game; but (2) a game where the imagined characters carry genuine worth, as do other aspects of the imagined world; and (3) a world-game where the worth of the imagined characters demands a cosmic context of fairness and, hence, a multiple-lives scheme.

Does this eastern vision suffice to explain and justify the dark sides of existence? Can it really make sense of the massive natural and human-caused evils?

The reader will have to judge.

No other type of vision, however, will give us a better shot at making sense of it all!

SELECTED BIBLIOGRAPHY

Almeder, Robert F. *Death and personal survival: the evidence for life after death*. Lanham, MD: Rowman & Littlefield, 1992.

Dostoevsky, Fyodor. *The Brothers Karamazov*. New York: Bantam Classics, 1984.

Grube, G.M.A. *Plato: The Republic*. Indianapolis: Hackett, 1992.

Kant, Immanuel. *Groundwork of the Metaphysic of Morals*, New York: Harper & Row, 1964.

Moody, Raymond. *Life after Life: the investigation of a phenomenon—survival of bodily death*, San Francisco: HarperSanFrancisco, 2001.

Nozick, Robert. *Anarchy, State, and Utopia*. New York: Basic Books, 1974.

Pirsig, R.M. *Zen and the Art of Motorcycle Maintenance*. London: Transworld, 1989.

Radhakrishnan, Sarvepalli, and Moore, Charles A. *A Source Book in Indian Philosophy*. Princeton: Princeton University Press, 1957.

Roberts, Jane. *The Nature of Personal Reality: A Seth Book*. Englewood Cliffs, N.J.: Prentice-Hall, 1974.

Rawls, John. *A Theory of Justice*. Cambridge: Harvard University Press, 1971.

Tillich, Paul. *The Eternal Now*. New York: Charles Scribner's Sons, 1963.